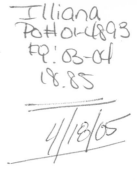

IN AMERICAN HISTORY

THE MISSION TRAILS IN AMERICAN HISTORY

(G) O

Carl R. Green

E **Enslow Publishers, Inc.**

40 Industrial Road   PO Box 38
Box 398   Aldershot
Berkeley Heights, NJ 07922 Hants GU12 6BP
USA   UK

http://www.enslow.com

This book is dedicated to my granddaughters Lauren, Beth, and Holly—talented travelers on a Royal Road to a bright and challenging future.

Library of Congress Cataloging-in-Publication Data

Green, Carl, R.
    The mission trails in American History / Carl R. Green.
        p. cm. — (In American history)
    Includes bibliographical references and index.
    Summary: Discusses the history and importance of the Chihuahua Trail, established in the sixteenth century to connect Mexico City and Santa Fe, and the Camino Real, established in the seventeenth century to take travelers and trade up the Californian coastline.
    ISBN 0-7660-1349-9
    1. Chihuahua Trail—History—Juvenile literature. 2. El Camino Real (Calif.)—History—Juvenile literature. 3. New Mexico—History—To 1848—Juvenile literature. 4. California—History—To 1846—Juvenile literature. 5. Frontier and pioneer life—New Mexico—Juvenile literature. 6. Frontier and pioneer life—California—Juvenile literature. [1. Chihuahua Trail—History. 2. El Camino Real (Calif.)—History. 3. New Mexico—History—To 1848. 4. California—History—To 1846.] I. Title: El Camino Real Trail in American history. II. Title. III. Series.
F799.G74   2001
978'.02—dc21

                                     99-462284

Printed in the United States of America

10 9 8 7 6 5 4 3 2 1

To Our Readers: We have done our best to make sure all Internet addresses in this book were active and appropriate when we went to press. However, the author and the publisher have no control over and assume no liability for the material available on those Internet sites or on other Web sites they may link to. Any comments or suggestions can be sent by e-mail to comments@enslow.com or to the address on the back cover.

Illustration Credits: Carl R. Green, pp. 15, 24, 27, 37, 40, 42, 52, 55, 60, 64, 67, 82(b), 105, 109, 111, 113; Courtesy of Donna Genet, p. 47; *DeskGallery MegaBundle*, Zedcor, Inc. and Dover Publications, Inc. (1995), p. 95; *Hastings' California Magazine*, p. 74; Library of Congress, p. 79; National Archives, pp. 7, 12, 19, 33, 100; Robert N. Mullin Collection, Haley Memorial Library, Midland, Texas, p. 70; *The American West in the Nineteenth Century*, Dover Publications, Inc. (1992), pp. 31, 58, 85, 86, 92, 98; Western History Department, Denver Public Library, p. 82(a).

Cover Illustrations: Carl R. Green; Library of Congress; National Archives; Robert N. Mullin Collection, Haley Memorial Library, Midland, Texas.

★ CONTENTS ★

When and where does American history begin? Some thoughtful people would say that the story begins with the continent's first inhabitants. In that case, the honors go to the ancestors of today's American Indians. Those early hunters and gatherers settled in North America some ten thousand years ago.

A COLLISION OF CULTURES

When it comes to European settlement, what about the Vikings who landed on the North Atlantic coast around A.D. 1000? Many grade school children would vote for the English colonists who landed in Virginia and Massachusetts in the early 1600s. Jamestown and Plymouth, after all, play major roles in most classroom history books.

For the most part, Americans tend to overlook the role played by Spanish explorers, soldiers, priests, and friars. Christopher Columbus opened the Age of Exploration when he first sighted land in the West Indies in 1492. By 1513 Juan Ponce de León was trekking across Florida. In 1521 Hernán Cortés conquered Mexico. Twenty years later, Francisco Vásquez de Coronado caught his first glimpse of the pueblos of

New Mexico. In 1596 the Spanish made a failed attempt to settle California. Two years later Juan de Oñate took possession of New Mexico in the name of his king. Spanish colonization was moving northward by leaps and bounds.

Spanish explorers often followed trails blazed by American Indian hunters and traders. Over the years, as more people traveled north and south, the rough tracks turned into well-marked roads. The main routes, which connected major cities, were known as royal roads—*los caminos reales*. One royal road, El Camino Real de Tierra Adentro, stretched from Mexico City, Mexico, to Santa Fe, New Mexico. This was the road that opened the Southwest to Spanish settlement. More than a century later, the Portolá-Serra expedition blazed a similar route up the California coastline. Known simply as El Camino Real, this new road earned an equally enduring place in western history.

In the late 1700s, the American colonists broke free of Great Britain and began looking westward. Settlers poured over trails such as the Wilderness Road into Kentucky, and the National Road into Ohio and Illinois. After crossing the Mississippi River they blazed the Oregon, California, and Santa Fe trails to points west. As the tide of settlement surged westward, traffic increased on the royal roads as well. El Camino Real de Tierra Adentro carried American merchants southward to markets in Chihuahua. During the Mexican War, El Camino Real played a key role in the struggle that brought California into the Union.

American Indians settled the Southwestern United States thousands of years before Europeans even dreamed of exploring the New World. Ancient artists left a record of their culture by carving images into sandstone boulders.

The Royal Highways carried more than friars, trade goods, soldiers, cattle, and settlers. Historians remind us that they also carried new ideas, customs, and technology. Only traces of the old roadways exist today, but their story lives on.

Pursuing a Ghost

In 1993, Douglas and Christine Preston set out to chase a ghost. Their phantom did not live in a haunted house or an old castle. The ghost they sought was that of the almost forgotten El Camino Real de Tierra

Adentro. Some four hundred years ago, this "Royal Road of the Interior" led Spanish soldiers, friars, and settlers north from Mexico City.

Most of the old route now lies buried beneath towns, highways, strip malls, and railroad tracks. The Prestons found traces of their ghost, however, in a desolate region north of El Paso, Texas. The years, they saw, had bypassed an area known as Lava Gate. "The landscape remained as it was in the thirteenth century when Pueblo Indians traded turquoise, salt, and macaws along this trail," they reported. "It was the same when the conquistador [conqueror] don Juan de Oñate rode through this gap in 1598 with a group of European colonists. It was the same when Kit Carson drove oxen down here in 1827. And it was still the same on July 16, 1945, when the terrible incandescence of the first atomic bomb, detonated only thirty-five miles away, illuminated this landscape."[1]

The Prestons experienced firsthand the dangers that El Camino Real de Tierra Adentro offered its travelers. On a whim, they drove their off-road vehicle down a dirt road toward the sand dunes of Samalayuca. After plowing through loose grit for ten miles, they reached the dunes—and stopped. Ahead lay row upon row of imposing sand hills. A brisk wind blew columns of sand off the top of the dunes. Small avalanches slid down the steep sides. The sight recalled the words of an American who had passed that way in 1848:

Ahead were the much-dreaded sand hills, . . . an immense field of steep sand ridges, without shrub or vegetation of any kind, looking like a piece of Arabian desert transplanted into this plain . . . In the meanwhile dark night had come on, illuminated only by lightning, that showed us for a while the most appalling night-scene—our wagons moving along as slow and solemn as a funeral procession; ghastly riders on horseback, wrapped in blankets or cloaks; . . . and the deepest silence interrupted only by the yelling exclamations of the drivers, and the rolling of distant thunder. . . . I made a vow the same night, that whenever I should undertake this trip again, I would rather go three days around, than travel once more over the sand hills with a wagon.[2]

Clearly, that long-ago gold seeker respected nature's awesome power. He likely did not know (or care) that he was walking in the footsteps of one of the Southwest's first explorers. Three hundred years earlier, Francisco Vázquez de Coronado led an expedition along that same route. Ahead, the explorer felt certain, lay the fabled Seven Cities of Cibola. Whoever found those towering cities of gold, the Spanish believed, would bring home wealth beyond imagination.

Coronado's Epic Journey

Coronado's journey into the unknown was inspired by a report from the dauntless Cabeza de Vaca. After surviving a shipwreck in Florida and capture by American Indians in Texas, de Vaca and several companions headed west on foot. Somewhere along the way, the men caught sight of what they thought was a distant city of gold. Once he reached safety in Mexico, de Vaca caught the attention of greedy officials with his vivid tales of Cibola's golden cities.

Only twenty years had passed since Hernán Cortés had conquered the Aztecs of Mexico. The splendid Aztec temples made it easy to believe in the Seven Cities. When he headed north into the American Southwest in 1540, Coronado led a force of 292 soldiers. Rounding out the party were friars, American Indian scouts and servants, and herds of horses, cattle, and sheep. As the expedition moved northward, the American Indians known as the Pueblo marveled at their first sight of men mounted on horseback. The Spanish, anxious to keep their advantage, did their best to keep their mounts to themselves. That policy broke down in the 1680s, when hundreds of horses ran free during the Pueblo Revolt. As the wild herds grew in size, the Navajo, Apache, and other tribes learned to tame and ride them.

Coronado sent soldiers to explore much of the Southwest, but his efforts to find the city of gold ended in failure. Cibola lived only in legend. What Coronado did find were the cliff-top pueblos built by the Zuni, Hopi, and other tribes. Viewed in the rays of the setting sun, the pueblo of Ácoma may well have gleamed with a golden light. This pueblo, the oldest inhabited settlement in the United States, stands high on a mesa (a flat, elevated area) east of Zuni, New Mexico. As Pedro de Castañeda described it, "The village was very strong . . . and so high that it was a very good musket that could throw a ball as high."[3]

At this point a guide told Coronado a tale that set Spanish pulses racing. In distant Quivira, he said, the fish in the river were as big as horses. The people, he claimed, ate from silver plates and drank from golden cups. In the spring of 1541 Coronado crossed the upper Rio Grande and headed into the Great Plains. He saw people who lived in teepees and hunted "wild cows"—the great herds of buffalo. But where was Quivira? After he reached Kansas and saw nothing but the grass lodges of the Wichitas, he turned back. The expedition had seen wonderful sights, including the Grand Canyon, but it was judged a failure. As Coronado wrote to the viceroy in Mexico City, "I must inform you of the good as well as the bad. . . . As far as I can judge, it does not appear to me that there is any hope of getting gold or silver."[4]

Cities of Clay, Not Gold

Had Coronado thought to look, he would have found a cultural treasure. The tribes of the upper Rio Grande were highly advanced. In an earlier age, their ancestors built great cliff cities on the high mesas of the region. Pueblo Bonito in New Mexico's Chaco Canyon counted eight hundred rooms and thirty-two kivas.[5] Kivas are round, mostly underground structures that the Pueblo people use for ceremonies. In the late 1200s, however, a long drought hit the region. The Pueblos (*pueblo* is Spanish for "village" or "town") were forced to leave

The nine-hundred-year-old Taos Pueblo may be the oldest occupied structure in the United States. Little has changed there since Spanish soldiers first sighted the sprawling structure in the 1540s.

their cliff dwellings. Starting over in the river valleys, the tribes built villages of timber and adobe clay. Story by story, builders added new rooms atop the old ones. Families entered their rooms through hatchways in the roofs. Ladders, which could be pulled up when danger threatened, led from one level to the next.

Game was scarce in a land where rainfall seldom topped twenty inches a year. The Pueblo met the challenge by planting crops in the bottom lands. Ditches and canals brought water to the fields. At harvest time the tribes filled their storage rooms with multicolored corn, beans, squash, cotton, and tobacco. Piñon trees yielded sweet nuts, and hunters stalked deer, bears, squirrels, and rabbits. The people dressed in garments woven from cotton and yucca fibers. Women decorated the clothing with turkey feathers and bits of shell and turquoise.

With their basic needs satisfied, the Pueblo turned to religion to enrich their lives. Group prayer, led by a holy man, was a cornerstone of everyday life. The people carried painted prayer sticks for protection and to confer blessings. On their way to the mountains, piñon nut gatherers asked for blessings on the harvest by stabbing prayer sticks into anthills. Back at the pueblo, religious groups met to dance and pray in the circular underground kivas. When they were preparing for a hunt, the dancers put on masks and sang to the animals. The songs assured the quarry that their lives would be taken only to feed hungry families. When enemies threatened the pueblo, the holy men sprinkled handfuls of sacred cornmeal around the walls.

In California, a Simpler Way of Life

During the Age of Conquest, the Spanish paid little attention to California. All their resources went into exploiting the vast treasures of Mexico and South America. After Sebastián Vizcaíno's 1602 voyage, nearly a century passed before the first settlement took root at Loreto in Baja California. As expeditions made their way northward, the soldiers and friars met

American Indians far different than the Pueblo of New Mexico.

Most California tribes lived by hunting and gathering. They did not farm, for the land supplied a bounty of food. The coastal dwellers ate nuts, berries, and shellfish, and made a nourishing meal from acorns. The men hunted deer with bow and arrow, but believed that anyone who killed a bear would fall ill or be driven insane. The early explorers were amazed to see that the men went naked or wore only a breechclout, a type of loincloth. The women dressed in aprons of shredded bark or deerskin.

Father Juan Crespí kept careful notes while he traveled up the coast in 1769. On October 23, his expedition stopped near a settlement of friendly American Indians. The village, he reported, contained a large grass-roofed house, surrounded by many little houses "of split sticks set upright." To welcome their guests, the villagers offered "large black-and white-colored tamales" made of acorn meal. Next came handfuls of wild tobacco, a gift that delighted the soldiers. The Spanish repaid their hosts by passing out handfuls of colored beads.[6]

California's American Indians lived peaceful lives. Brief wars sometimes flared when one tribe trespassed on land claimed by another. The women made colorful, watertight baskets and decorated them with shell beads and bright feathers. After living in their grass huts for several months, they cleaned house by burning the huts. A fire always burned in the village *temescal*, or

Simple reed huts known as kiitchas *sheltered California's American Indians from rain and sun. To prepare one of their basic foods, the women pounded acorns into a meal in stones hollowed out by years of use.*

sweat lodge. When the men who gathered there were steaming hot, they ran out and dove into the ocean, a lake, or a stream.

Visions and magic were important to tribal religious beliefs. During a boy's passage into adulthood, the elders helped him conjure up spirit visions by feeding him a potent tea made from jimsonweed. Many of the tribes burned their dead—along with the dead person's house and belongings. Until the fire had done its work, no one risked a visit from unfriendly spirits by speaking the name of the deceased. Because the people did not have a written language, elders passed on religious beliefs and tribal history by word of mouth. The Yokut children of the San Joaquin Valley surely felt better after reciting this eloquent prayer:

Do you see me!

See me, Tüüshiut!

See me, Pamashiut!

See me, Yuhahait!

See me, Eshepat!

See me, Pitsuriut!

See me, Tsuksit!

See me, Ukat!

Do you all help me!

My words are tied in one

With the great mountains,

With the great rocks,

With the great trees,

In one with my body

And my heart.

Do you all help me

With supernatural power

And you, day,

And you, night!

All of you see me

One with this world.[7]

Blazing a Trail Northward

California's American Indians might have prayed harder if they had known what the future held. All during the 1500s, the Spanish moved slowly northward from their base in Mexico City. Spurred by the opening of rich silver mines, soldiers carved out a road some called Camino de la Plata (the Silver Road). Year by year, the rough wagon track pushed farther north. By 1580 this royal road stretched 850 miles north to Chihuahua. For some twenty years the frontier ended there. Settlers lived on lonely ranches or took refuge in scattered mining camps, small towns, and *presidios* (military posts). Many fell victim to the desert heat or to American Indian raiding parties angered by the sight of newcomers moving in on their lands.

In 1581 three friars and their soldier escorts pushed north into New Mexico. The friars came as missionaries, charged with converting the natives to Christianity. After the soldiers returned home, word came that the friars were in danger. Antonio de Espéjo mounted a rescue expedition, but he arrived too late to save the luckless friars. Determined to make the trip worthwhile, Espéjo retraced portions of Coronado's route and explored the Rio Grande valley. The report he delivered to Mexico City described the land in glowing terms. Spanish officials took note. The time had come, they declared, to send settlers into what Espéjo called the Kingdom of New Mexico.[8]

★ MESA VERDE: HOME OF THE ANCIENT ONES ★

Some hikers stumble upon an empty house while walking in the woods. Taking a deep breath, they step through the half-open door and look around. Are there any clues to help reconstruct the daily life of the family that once lived there? At first, it seems there are only cobwebs and decay. Then, in a back room, they find three plastic bags stuffed with . . . rubbish! If the hikers were archeologists (scientists who study ancient cultures), they would be overjoyed.

Archeologists dig into the "trash" (they call their artifacts) left by people who lived long ago. One of the richest archeological sites in the United States is at Mesa Verde in southwestern Colorado. There, a resourceful people known as the Anasazi (the ancient ones) settled about A.D. 550. For some six hundred years, the Anasazi lived and farmed on the flat top of the mesa. Then, around 1200, the Anasazi reacted to the arrival of the Navajo and Apache by rebuilding their villages in the walls of the nearby cliffs. Thanks to solid construction and a dry climate, the cliff dwellings have survived the ravages of time.

Around 1275, a long drought and killing frosts shriveled crops all across the Southwest. The Anasazi left Mesa Verde and vanished from history. Archeologists believe that the people scattered as they moved into the fertile valleys of the Rio Grande, Gila, and Salt rivers. Traces of their influence, from pottery to farming methods, show up in Pueblo culture. Most of what we know about them, however, depends on artifacts found at sites such as Mesa Verde National Park.

Two cowboys stumbled onto Mesa Verde's cliff dwellings in 1888 while searching for lost cattle. As the

This 1873 photo captures a quiet moment in the life of a Navajo family in New Mexico's Canyon de Chelle. At left, a Navajo man prepares his bow for a hunting trip. Beside him, his wife concentrates on her weaving.

news spread, visitors prowled the ruins and carried off pottery shards and other "souvenirs." To protect the site, Congress in 1906 passed a bill that turned Mesa Verde into a national park. Along with its historic value, the site has other lessons to teach. Experts agree that several factors drove the cliff dwellers away from Mesa Verde. The most important were probably population pressures, depleted resources, tribal conflicts, and a changing climate. As writer Caroline Arnold reminds us, these are "the same issues that we face today on a global level. The plight of the Anasazi illustrates how important it is to use one's resources wisely and how a slight shift in climate can change a good life to a marginal existence."[9]

DURING THE SAME YEAR [1538] THE FATHER PROVINCIAL
SENT TWO OTHER RELIGIOUS [TWO FRIARS] BY LAND ALONG
THE SAME COAST OF THE SOUTH SEA, TRAVELING
NORTHWARD THROUGH JALISCO AND NUEVA GALICIA
[SINALOA, MEXICO]. . . . ONE OF THE TWO RELIGIOUS
BECAME ILL AND . . . TURNED BACK; AND THE OTHER . . .
CONTINUED ON THE LEFT-HAND ROAD TOWARD THE COAST, A
VERY STRAIGHT ROAD. HE ARRIVED AT A LAND INHABITED BY
POOR INDIANS WHO CAME OUT TO RECEIVE THE PRIEST,
BELIEVING HIM TO BE SOMETHING FROM HEAVEN. . . . THEY
FIRST GAVE FOOD TO THE PRIEST SO THAT HE MIGHT EAT, AND
THE REST THEY DIVIDED AMONG THEMSELVES. AND SO, IN
THIS WAY, HE TRAVELED MORE THAN 200 LEAGUES.[10]

* * * * *

[O]N THE THIRD DAY AFTER HE BADE HIS BROTHER
COMPANIONS FAREWELL, [FRAY JUAN DE SANTA MARÍA]
WENT TO TAKE A NAP UNDER A TREE, AND THE TIGUAS
INDIANS, . . . KILLED HIM AND BURNED HIS BONES. THE
OTHER TWO PRIESTS RETURNED TO THE PUEBLO OF PUARAY,
. . . ENJOYING GOOD, FRIENDLY TREATMENT. THEY STAYED
THERE WITH THE INDIANS, LEARNING THEIR LANGUAGE,
UNTIL THE DEVIL, BEING OUR ENEMY, PLAYED HIS TRICKS.
ONE AFTERNOON, WHILE FRAY FRANCISCO LÓPEZ WAS
PRAYING, . . . AN INDIAN KILLED HIM WITH TWO BLOWS OF A
WAR CLUB THAT STRUCK HIM ON THE TEMPLES. . . . THE
CAPTAIN OF THE PUEBLO SHOWED SIGNS OF SORROW. . . .
[B]UT IN AN UNMINDFUL MOMENT, THE INDIANS CAME AND
[KILLED] FRAY AGUSTÍN RUIZ ALSO, AND THREW HIS BODY
INTO THE RIVER.[11]

*Father Gerónimo de Zárate Salmerón lived and
worked in New Mexico from 1621 to 1626. Along
with his religious duties, the Franciscan friar wrote a
history of the region. In the second reading, the men
who died were friars who came to New Mexico to
attempt to convert natives.*

2

"OH GOD! WHAT A LONELY LAND!"

In the spring of 1598, a Spanish caravan straggled northward across the Chihuahua desert. When the settlers reached the Rio Grande, they set up camp near the site of modern El Paso, Texas. There the weary settlers rested and prayed that the long journey soon would be over. Their captain general, a nobleman named Juan de Oñate, studied the terrain beyond the river. It was time to begin the immense task of turning New Mexico into a prosperous colony.

On April 30, Oñate stepped forward and raised his arms to the sky. "I take possession, once, twice, and thrice," he proclaimed, "of the lands of the said Río del Norte [Rio Grande], . . . with all its meadows and pasture grounds and passes . . . and all other lands, pueblos, cities, villas, of whatsoever nature now founded in the kingdom and province of New Mexico."[1] His soldiers then nailed a cross to a tree and planted a flag next to the river. The fact that they were claiming land that belonged to American Indian tribes did not trouble the Spanish.

The ceremonies ended, the caravan resumed its trek. The heavy carts cut deep ruts into the sandy soil. Those tracks marked the route that travelers would later know as El Camino Real de Tierra Adentro.

A Harsh and Demanding Landscape

The Royal Highway grew ever longer as the expedition trudged northward. In time the route from Mexico City to Santa Fe covered some 1,600 miles. For many years it ranked as the longest road built by Europeans in North America. For the most part, the desert terrain was hostile to these newcomers. Travelers often echoed the words of the observer who wrote, "Oh God! What a lonely land!"[2]

The Spanish tended to follow trails left by American Indians. Mainly they chose flat terrain that led from one water source to the next. Good water meant there would be grass for livestock and firewood for cooking. Finding a long-sought river was a welcome event, but crossing it posed fresh challenges. After watering their horses, scouts fanned out to search for fords where the footing was secure and the current was slow. Building the rafts needed to float cargo across flooded rivers slowed progress and strained tempers.

El Camino Real de Tierra Adentro challenged travelers at nearly every step. From an elevation of 7,800 feet at Mexico City, the road fell to 4,709 feet at Chihuahua. After descending a thousand feet to El Paso, wagon trains bound for Santa Fe had to climb to over 7,000 feet. Along the way the road snaked through grasslands, deserts, and cottonwood forests. In the lowlands the temperature soared during the summer and dropped below freezing in winter. Altitude made Santa Fe more livable, with an average low of 32°F (0°C) and an average high of 70°F (21°C). The deserts often went years without rain. Cloudbursts in the uplands, however, could send floodwaters surging down the Rio Grande.

At no time in those early years did the road look like a modern highway. Douglas Preston describes El

Bypassed by modern highways, a Mexican village keeps alive the memory of El Camino Real de Tierra Adentro. Over the centuries, travelers have worn the roadbed down to a level several feet below the nearby fields.

Camino Real as a long, twisted braid. "There were shortcuts and longcuts," he writes, "rough trails for pack trains and smoother roads for *carretas* (carts), drier routes and wetter routes, harsher routes and gentler routes."[3] Caravans took one route in wet months, and another during times of drought. The favorite stopping points, known as *parajes*, provided water, grass, and wood. When game was scarce, travelers slaughtered a cow or a goat from the herds they brought with them.

The Spanish stretched the supplies of bacon, flour, and beans they carried in their carts by hunting along the way. The grasslands nurtured black-tailed jackrabbits and pronghorn antelope. Desert scrub supported mule deer, desert cottontails, bighorn sheep, and quail. The river valleys swarmed with sandhill cranes, ducks, geese, wild turkey, and bears. The hunter who brought down a black bear was hero for a day. The meat was tasty, the fur was warm, and the fat could be used to grease squeaky axles. In time, overhunting all but wiped out the mule deer and several other species.

The toughest part of the journey lay north of El Paso. At a point where the Rio Grande loops westward, mountains barred the way. The alternate route was a ninety-mile stretch of desert known as La Jornada del Muerto. To make this well-named Journey of the Dead, wagon trains moved out in the early evening and traveled at night. A twenty-five-mile march ended at Laguna del Muerto—the Lake of the Dead—but all too often the lake was dry. Juan de

Oñate's party found one of the much-treasured water holes on the Jornada because a dog returned to camp with muddy feet. In tribute to that stroke of luck, the waterhole was called Ojo del Perrillo—the Spring of the Little Dog.[4]

Another of the region's landmarks is the Fra Cristóbal mountain range. The low, rocky peaks, named for a saintly friar who traveled with Oñate, rise between the Rio Grande and La Jornada del Muerto. After baptizing many Pueblo children, Father Cristóbal de Salazar headed back to Mexico to recruit more settlers. After he died on the way, his companions buried him at the foot of the mountains that now bear his name. Before long, travelers were telling a strange story. They had seen the face of Father Cristóbal, they said, in the contours of those barren mountains.

Blazing a New Road into the Wilderness

The first ill-fated efforts to colonize New Mexico collapsed in the 1580s. When royal officials decided to try again, they handed the job to Juan de Oñate. Volunteers heard the wealthy soldier's call and hurried to join him. When the column at last rumbled north in 1598, Oñate rode at the head of hundreds of men, women, and children. All knew they might never return. Visions of fame, royal favor, land grants, and mineral wealth drew them onward.

The expedition was well planned. The livestock herd contained seven thousand cattle and numerous horses, mules, and oxen. Each morning drivers hitched the slow-footed oxen to eighty-three two-wheeled wagons, carts, and carriages. Once it was under way, the column stretched nearly two miles from the first cart to the last. The carts carried food, clothing, armor, and household goods. Hoping to put on a good show for the Pueblo, Oñate also packed his velvet suits and plumed hats.[5]

Oñate proved his courage early in the journey. Finding the Río Conchos in full flood, he spurred his horse into the current and splashed to the far bank. Heartened by this reckless act, his followers plunged in after him. Thirty miles further on, after crossing the

In the early days of the trail, wooden carts were used to haul supplies north from Mexico City to Spanish missions. The carts groaned and rattled over the rough roads, but they were cheap to make and easy to repair.

Río San Pedro, Oñate again took the more direct route. Instead of circling far to the east to avoid Chihuahua's trackless wasteland, he dispatched scouts to find a trail that led due north. Guided by the faint tracks left by American Indian hunters, the scouts found a way through to the Rio Grande. The trail they blazed became an important segment of El Camino Real de Tierra Adentro.

Led by the scouts, the expedition plodded from one water hole to the next. The shifting sand dunes of Los Médanos provided the next great test. The settlers conquered the deep sand by hitching four oxen to each cart. After pulling half the carts through, the drivers led the oxen back and repeated the process. By the time the column reached the Rio Grande, people and animals were nearly crazed with thirst. One observer noted that men who drank too much river water swelled up "like toads."[6]

After the formal ceremonies at the Rio Grande, Oñate was ready to push into New Mexico. Friendly American Indians helped him across the river at a shallow ford, and he stayed close to the river as he led the way northward. Only when mountains and arroyos (ravines) blocked the way did he take the trail across La Jornada del Muerto. Oñate and his soldiers made the crossing at night, leaving the slow-moving carts to follow behind.

On his way north Oñate stopped at a number of pueblos. At each village he promised to protect the people if they swore loyalty to the crown and embraced the Christian faith. At the point where the Chama River flows into the Rio Grande, he found a wide, fertile valley and a pueblo known as O'ke. Oñate drove out the inhabitants and proclaimed the site as his capital. As a tribute to his horsemen, he named the settlement San Juan de los Caballeros. Five weeks later the slow-moving carts caught up with the advance guard.

Despite his best efforts, Oñate soon lost control of his "kingdom." The land did not yield its riches easily, and hunger stalked the small settlement. Instead of dealing with the problem, Oñate spent much of his time exploring his domain. During one of his absences, a group of colonists packed up and returned to Mexico. The viceroy—the governor-general of New Spain—listened to their tale of woe and dispatched a new provincial governor. After he replaced Oñate, Pedro de Peralta moved the capital to a safer, more central site at Santa Fe. El Camino Real de Tierra Adentro was nearly complete.

Traveling a Long Road

Anyone who set out to travel the route north from Mexico City faced an exhausting six-month trek. Even so, New Mexico's missions and settlements had to be supplied. All through the 1600s, wagon trains headed northward at intervals that ranged from three to seven years. Friars sent to do missionary work carried food, clothing, kitchen gear, medicines, and church vestments.

To prepare for saying mass, each friar carted in the following supplies:

- 2½ pounds of incense
- 2½ pounds of copal [a resin used as incense]
- Three ounces of silk wicking to make candles
- Three pesos' worth of soap for washing ceremonial robes
- One missal [prayer book] and three books of chants
- 45 gallons of sacramental wine
- 85½ pounds of prepared candle wax
- 26 gallons of lamp oil for illuminating the altar[7]

A typical supply train was made up of thirty-two wagons, each pulled by eight mules. A Franciscan friar supervised the thirty-two drivers, the American Indian scouts and slaves, and the military escort. Merchants, traders, and government officials often joined the supply train for the trip. They believed that the sight of a large, well-armed caravan would keep Apache and Navajo raiders from launching an attack.

The stout, four-wheeled wagons used in the caravans looked like the Conestogas that carried America's settlers westward two hundred years later. Each groaned under the weight of two tons of cargo or more. Alert to the dangers of breakdowns, packers added spare axles, spokes, harness, and mule shoes to the load. As a sign of the supply train's official status, the lead wagons flew banners bearing the royal coat of arms. On the journey north, the wagons plunged into the wilderness after leaving Santa Bárbara. The next supply point lay hundreds of miles away at the Rio Grande. After resting there, the footsore travelers

A new governor moved New Mexico's capitol to Santa Fe in the early 1600s. Over two centuries later, when this engraving was made, the bustling settlement was served by two major trails—El Camino Real de Tierra Adentro and the Santa Fe Trail.

trudged on to the church's headquarters at Santo Domingo. Smaller supply trains rolled on from there to the outlying missions and to Santa Fe.

Four months later, the wagon train reassembled to begin the return trip. This time the wagons sagged under the weight of products from New Mexico's missions, ranches, and mines. The settlers paid for the goods sent from Mexico with piñon nuts, antelope and buffalo hides, wheat, corn, raw wool, cowhides, and salt. In 1821, with the opening of the Santa Fe Trail, the United States hurried to join the lively trade. By then Mexico had thrown off Spanish rule, and a new Royal Highway was flourishing on the Pacific coast.

★ THE PUEBLO REVOLT AND RECONQUEST ★

At first the Pueblo welcomed the newcomers who arrived on El Camino Real. As the months passed, Spanish demands for tribute (paid in labor and products) fractured that relationship. At the same time, famine and disease stalked the land. Navajo and Apache raiders compounded the misery by striking hard at the weakened villages. Dismayed by their ill future, many of the Pueblo turned back to the worship of their tribal gods.

In 1675, Governor Treviño took alarm at this rebirth of "superstition." On his orders, soldiers rounded up forty-seven tribal medicine men. A church court convened in Santa Fe and tried them on charges of witchcraft. Of the four who were found guilty, one killed himself in his cell. The Spanish hung the other three in public as a lesson to their fellow villagers. The remaining leaders were either locked up or given a public flogging. This harsh punishment brought a warning from the Pueblo nations. Free the prisoners, the tribal leaders told Treviño, or we will kill you and all your people.[8]

At the time fewer than three thousand settlers lived in New Mexico. Treviño had no choice but to release the medicine men. One of them, a fiery mystic named Popé, began calling for an uprising to drive out the Spanish. His only hope of success, he knew, was to unite all the tribes in his cause. When he announced that the Pueblo gods approved the revolt, the Pueblo people listened and believed. To keep their plans secret, Popé's followers killed anyone suspected of talking to the Spanish.

The plan worked all too well. Pueblo war parties attacked the Spanish settlements on August 10, 1680. In the first chaotic days the vengeful warriors killed twenty-one friars and some four hundred men, women, and

Spanish friars did their best to erase all traces of the traditional American Indian religions. Yet, the old ways survived, as this 1879 photo of Zuni "Mud Heads" confirms. These elders are gathering to prepare for a ceremonial dance.

children. They also burned houses and drove off livestock. Santa Fe fell after a bloody siege and the governor joined his fellow survivors as they fled south on El Camino Real. The refugees came to rest at El Paso, leaving New Mexico in the hands of the Pueblo.

In the next dozen years, the Spanish made several futile efforts to reconquer the province. Success came in 1692, after Pueblo unity broke down under the twin pressures of drought and raids by Navajo and Apache war parties. To recapture the province, Don Diego de Vargas led two hundred soldiers north on El Camino Real. All along the way, the villages stood empty, deserted in the face of the oncoming troops. At the capital, Vargas parlayed with the Pueblos who held the town. His show of force, coupled with the promise of fair treatment, opened the gates and avoided a battle for the city.

Although the fighting dragged on for four more years, the worst was over. Today some historians credit the Pueblo people with conducting the colonial period's only successful American Indian revolt.

LETTER TO THE VICEROY
OCTOBER 1, 1601

WHO, THEN IS TO BLAME, IF NOT OUR SINS, FOR THE BAD LUCK THAT OUR SERVICES AND LABORS HAVE PROFITED US SO LITTLE? ALL WILL BE LOST IF OUR LORD DOES NOT REMEDY THIS SITUATION BY PERMITTING THE GOVERNOR TO DISCOVER SOMETHING SO IMPORTANT THAT THE MEN MAY OVERCOME THEIR INDIFFERENCE AND LACK OF CONFIDENCE IN FINDING ANYTHING WORTHWHILE IN THESE LANDS. . . . IF SUCCOR DOES NOT REACH US WITHIN FIVE MONTHS WE WILL BE COMPELLED TO ABANDON THIS LAND, AS WE ARE DETERMINED TO DO. WE AGAIN ASK YOUR EXCELLENCY TO FAVOR US SINCE WE HAVE SERVED HIS MAJESTY FOR SIX YEARS IN THIS EXPEDITION, TOGETHER WITH OUR WIVES, CHILDREN, AND FAMILIES, AND HAVE SPENT LARGE AMOUNTS OF OUR ESTATES. OUR GREATEST SACRIFICE HAS BEEN THE LOSS OF LIBERTY, WHICH WE HUMBLY ASK YOUR EXCELLENCY TO RESTORE, AND WHICH WE HOLD AS THE MOST TREASURED REWARD FOR OUR HARDSHIP.
—LIEUTENANT GOVERNOR DON FRANCISCO DE SOSA PEÑALOSA[9]

By 1601 the colonists who had followed Juan de Oñate to New Mexico were giving up hope. The "loss of liberty" refers to the fact that no one was allowed to leave without royal permission. A few years later, with the colony well established, the pleas were for iron tools and horseshoes. "We are perishing," a resident of Santa Fe wrote, "without a pound of iron or a plough."[10]

A New Road in a New Land

Father Junípero Serra's heart soared as his mule jogged down to the lonely Pacific coastline. It was a sunny June day in 1769. The long, hard journey north from Loreto in Baja California was over at last. Ahead he could see the masts of two sailing ships lying at anchor in the sheltered bay. The ships, he knew, carried the men and supplies he needed to begin the task of bringing the Christian faith to Alta California.

Serra's joy soon vanished. Many of the sailors had died of scurvy during the long voyage. In that age no one knew that adding fruits and vegetables rich in vitamin C to the sailors' diet would prevent the deadly disease. Serra was forced to draw on his immense store of courage and faith. When he wrote to a friend, he expressed his thanks to God for guiding him to the beautiful bay. Despite the many setbacks, the settlement of upper California was under way.

Years of Exploration and Neglect

Some twenty years before Father Serra reached San Diego, a new map went on sale in parts of Europe.

Except for the modern fence, this arid California hillside looks much the same as it did when the Spanish passed through in the early 1770s. For the most part the friars and soldiers kept to the valleys and coastal plains in order to bypass the more rugged stretches.

One section showed a large land mass lying off the west coast of North America. The mapmaker called the island California, a name drawn from a popular novel of the early 1500s. In *The Exploits of Esplandián*, Garcí Ordóñez de Montalvo had described the land as home to a race of black-skinned Amazon women. Ruling over this golden realm was the noble Queen Calafía. It turned out that Calafía lived only in the writer's imagination. Her memory, however, survives in the name given to her island—California.[1]

The first European to set foot on the "island" was Fortún Jiménez, who landed at the tip of the long peninsula known as Baja California in 1533. Instead of finding gold and Amazons, Jiménez found an early grave. The local American Indians killed the explorer and twenty of his men. The survivors hastily weighed anchor and sailed back to Mexico. Fresh from his conquest of Mexico, Hernán Cortés landed in the same area two years later. Finding little to enrich the royal treasury, he did not stay long.

The honor of first setting foot on the coast of Alta California fell to Juan Rodríguez Cabrillo. Cabrillo landed at San Diego Bay in 1542 and then sailed north. After a stop at Catalina Island, he crossed to the mainland and anchored at a harbor he called La Bahía de los Fumos (the Bay of Smokes). The smoke came from the cooking fires of the Gabrieliño Indians—and a city named Los Angeles later took root there. Hampered by a broken arm, Cabrillo pushed as far north as San Francisco Bay before bad weather forced him to turn back. The badly set arm became infected, and Cabrillo died while his ship was anchored at San Miguel Island. His second in command, Bartolomé Ferrelo, took the helm and sailed as far as the Oregon coast before heading back to Mexico.

Ferrelo's reports of what he saw fell on mostly deaf ears. Spread thin by global expansion, Spain lacked the resources to send settlers to California. In 1602, Sebastián Vizcaíno almost tipped the balance. The explorer vastly oversold the value of the bay he found while exploring the northern California coast. "[Monterey Bay] is all that can be desired as a harbor for ships making the voyage from the Philippines," he reported.[2] That touched off a brief surge of interest in planting a colony at Monterey, but the costs were too great. The dream had to be put on hold.

In 1683 Father Eusebio Francisco Kino opened the way to settlement when he founded a mission at the tip of Baja California. After the tiny colony collapsed, Kino set out to explore the unmapped territory to the north. From the modern-day Arizona border, Kino and his American Indian guides blazed a new trail west to the Colorado River. In years to come desert-weary travelers would dub it El Camino del Diablo (the Devil's Road). After crossing the great Red River, Kino saw the gulf coast continue to the south. The sight proved what he had already guessed. *"California no es isla"* (California is not an island), he wrote.[3]

After an interlude in Mexico, Kino returned to Baja in 1697. Equipped with supplies paid for by wealthy patrons, he set up a base near the midpoint of the peninsula. From his new town of Loreto, Kino hoped to build a road that would connect with San Diego and Monterey. When he died in 1711, the southern arm of the road was nearing La Paz. The much longer northern route was still a dream.

The Trek North: Loreto to San Diego

Nearly sixty years passed before events conspired to open the way to Alta California. In 1767, convinced

 (map showing EL CAMINO REAL; *The King's Highways Lead Northward*; El Camino Real de Tierra Adentro 1540-1610; El Camino Real, Baja California to Sonoma, 1769-1823)

The torturous routes that carried Spanish soldiers, friars, and colonists northward from Mexico were known as Los Caminos Reales—the King's Highways. The older road from Mexico City to Santa Fe later became known as El Camino Real de Tierra Adentro.

that Jesuit friars were abusing their power, King Charles III ordered them to leave the New World. To carry on their missionary work, he turned to a second holy order, the Franciscans. At the same time, word reached Spain that Russian fur traders and British warships had been sighted in northern California. This worried the king's advisors, who feared that Spain's rivals would annex the strategic territory. Orders went out to "guard the dominions from all invasion and insult."[4]

The Franciscans gave Father Junípero Serra the task of managing the Baja missions. Almost as soon as he took up his post, new orders came through. The king's agent, José de Gálvez, was organizing an expedition to colonize Alta California. Unlike most of his fellow officials, Gálvez was a man of vision. At one time, for example, he had toyed with the idea of training apes to be used as soldiers.[5] Now he threw himself into what proved to be another knotty problem. To handle the missionary chores for the new colony, Gálvez sent for Serra. To lead the expedition, he chose Baja's governor, Gaspár de Portolá. Both men were delighted. Serra hungered to minister to a people he thought were uncivilized and godless. Portolá, bored with his duties, buckled on a sword and embarked on his great adventure.

Early in 1769 the *San Carlos* sailed for California with a cargo of food and soldiers. A month later the *San Antonio* followed. Bedeviled by headwinds and faulty maps, both ships missed San Diego Bay on their first pass. By the time they found their way back to the harbor, sailors were dying of scurvy. A third ship vanished, never to be heard from again. The disasters convinced Gálvez that the venture would succeed only if the settlements were linked by a road.

Back at the Loreto mission, two pack trains prepared to march north across mountains of "stones and

The missions and ranchos established by the early Californios depended on cattle herds for income. Using the same tools as his ancestors, this leatherworker prepares a hide for tanning.

thorns." The first column took two months to travel the 350 miles to San Diego. Captain Portolá and Father Serra led the second pack train when it left Loreto in mid-May. Serra was slowed by a painful ulcer on his leg. When nothing else worked, he smeared his leg with an ointment used to treat the mules' saddle sores. The treatment relieved the pain, but Serra and his companions were facing a greater threat. Food supplies ran short, forcing the party to live off the land. The American Indian guides "joyfully ate" a mule that an angry cook had killed because the clumsy animal had stumbled. To punish the cook for killing a valuable pack animal, Portolá forced him to walk the rest of the way.[6]

The joy of reaching San Diego was tempered by bad news for the friars. Sailors were dying, and many of the American Indian slaves had escaped. The leaders took the setbacks in stride. Portolá's first act as Governor of Alta California was to send the *San Antonio* back to Mexico for supplies. Then, as Serra began building Mission San Diego de Alcalá, he prepared for the trek to Monterey. On a hot July day Portolá led a troop of "skeletons who had been spared by scurvy, hunger, and thirst" on their epic journey.[7]

The Trek North: San Diego to Monterey

Sixty-four soldiers, muleteers, and two friars followed Portolá into the heavy underbrush. One of the friars was Father Juan Crespí, a boyhood friend of Father

Serra. An officer and eight soldiers used spades and crowbars to clear a trail for the pack train. Portolá set an easy pace that covered just six miles per day. As one officer noted, "Camp was pitched early each afternoon so that the explorers could scout ahead. . . . More protracted halts were called after unusually fatiguing marches, or if a stampede necessitated recovery of the animals."[8]

One of the roundups took place as the column neared the modern site of Los Angeles. Horses and mules stampeded when a "terrible earthquake" shook the ground. A few days later, as they crossed the plain below the Hollywood Hills, Portolá found "springs of tar, or pitch, boiling up out of the ground."[9] Today, scientists know that popular tourist site as the La Brea tar pits.

The column followed the path of least resistance. From Los Angeles the way led through the oak-shaded San Fernando Valley. Then it slowly veered westward. When he reached the Santa Barbara Channel, Portolá recognized landmarks described by Cabrillo over two hundred years earlier. A local tribe known as the Canaleños welcomed the Spaniards and showed them bits of metal left by earlier visitors. Later travelers would abuse the tribe's trust in white men, but for now all was peaceful. Portolá asked for—and received—help in finding the best route north. The Spanish made more friends at San Luis Obispo. On Portolá's orders, his men shot several grizzly bears that had been terrorizing a native village.

On September 16, 1769, the Sierra de Santa Lucia mountains blocked the expedition's path. With supplies running low, the men searched for a ridge they could follow north. The beauty of the scene was lost on the weary party. As Father Crespí wrote, it was "a sad outlook for poor travelers, tired and worn by the fatigues of the journey, by the task of clearing rough passages and breaking roads through hills, woods, dunes and swamps."[10] By the time they reached the Salinas River, some of the men were too weak to go on. Portolá ordered the others to strap their companions to wooden frames so the mules could carry them.

Step by slow step, the men plodded northward. Any day now, Portolá felt certain, they would reach the port Vizcaíno had described. Instead of a "port sheltered from all winds," the bay they found at Monterey was open to every passing storm. As Portolá wrote, "What should have been a seaport is only a little cove."[11] Scouting parties probed further north, only to run into an arm of San Francisco Bay. Vizcaíno, it seemed clear, had vastly overrated his find. To mark their arrival, the soldiers set up a large cross on the shore.

Portolá, weakened by scurvy, ordered his men to retrace their steps. For several weeks, the southbound column lived on foul-smelling mule meat. Below Point Concepción, however, the weather improved. Friendly tribes gave the travelers wholesome food. At last, four months after leaving Monterey, the column made it back to Serra's crude mission. As they recovered their strength, the men took pride in their feat—the first round trip over a new Royal Highway.

★ FATHER JUNÍPERO SERRA: THE ROAD TO SAINTHOOD ★

He called himself the Gray Ox. History calls him "Father of the California Missions." Sometime soon, if church officials can confirm one more miracle to their satisfaction, the Catholic Church will call him a saint—Saint Junípero Serra.

The Blessed Serra (his current church title) was born on the Spanish island of Mallorca in 1713. His parents, true to their Catholic faith, sent the boy to a school run by Franciscan monks. There, at age sixteen, he chose a life of service to the church. After he was ordained as a priest, his superiors divided his time between the pulpit and the classroom. For a time Serra was content to encourage his students to volunteer for missionary work. As time passed, however, he felt the call to "place the gentle yoke of Christ" on non-Christian peoples. In 1749, he said farewell to Spain and boarded a ship bound for Mexico.

The sturdy Franciscan inspired everyone with his zeal. To prove that he would never take the easy way, he walked the 150 miles from Veracruz to Mexico City. Along the way an infected spider bite developed into a painful ulcer. Walking or riding became a torture, but Serra pressed on. For the next eighteen years he served throughout Mexico, walking at least 6,000 miles in pursuit of his duties. It was here that he took to calling himself the Gray Ox. Like his namesake beast of burden, he plodded on, seeming never to tire.

Between 1769 and 1784, Father Junípero Serra tirelessly forged the first links in a chain of missions that stretched from San Diego in the south to Sonoma in the north. This statue of Serra is located at Mission Santa Barbara.

In 1768, José de Gálvez picked Serra to carry on the church's work in California. Still hobbled by the festering ulcer, Serra tackled his new job with a youthful zeal. At first he guided the work of the thirteen missions the Jesuits had built in Baja California. His heart, however, lay in the task of bringing God to Alta California. After arriving at San Diego in 1769, he built the first of his nine missions along El Camino Real. His followers added twelve more missions to the chain after he died in 1784.

Father Serra's unflagging spirit laid the foundation for much of California's later growth. The story of this saintly holy man does have its dark side, however. Serra blessed the coastal tribes as "free and alive"—but for many, life at the missions meant a loss of freedom. When they were exposed to diseases such as measles and syphilis, the American Indian population dwindled to near extinction. Serra, for all his goodness, did not seem to realize the danger. "I do for them what I can, caress them as I may," he wrote, "—And thus we journey onward."[12]

OCTOBER 8 [1769]. I NAMED THIS PLACE THE RIVER OF SANTA ANA [THE PRESENT-DAY PAJARO RIVER, NEAR WATSONVILLE], A VERY FINE PLACE FOR A VERY LARGE MISSION, WITH A GREAT DEAL OF SOIL AND WATER FOR IRRIGATING IT, AND A GREAT AMOUNT OF TIMBER. FOR BESIDES THE MANY GOOD-SIZED COTTONWOODS ON THE RIVER, THERE BEGINS HERE A LARGE MOUNTAIN RANGE COVERED WITH A TREE VERY LIKE THE PINE IN ITS LEAF, SAVE THAT THIS IS NOT OVER TWO FINGERS LONG. THE HEARTWOOD IS RED, VERY HANDSOME WOOD, HANDSOMER THAN CEDAR. NO ONE KNEW WHAT KIND OF WOOD IT MIGHT BE; IT MAY BE SPRUCE, WE CANNOT TELL. MANY SAID SAVIN, AND SAVIN 'TWAS CALLED, THOUGH I HAVE NEVER SEEN THEM RED. THERE ARE GREAT NUMBERS OF THIS TREE HERE, OF ALL SIZES OF THICKNESS, MOST OF THEM EXCEEDINGLY HIGH AND STRAIGHT LIKE SO MANY CANDLES. WHAT A PLEASURE TO SEE THIS BLESSING OF TIMBER.

—*FATHER JUAN CRESPÍ*[13]

Father Crespí kept a faithful record of the sights he saw while trekking north with Gaspár de Portolá in 1769. He was looking ahead to a day when new missions would arise all along the route. By the time he died in 1782, nine of those missions were open. The tall trees that Crespí admired were coast redwoods, close cousins to the giant sequoias. These few sentences are thought to be the first mention of the redwoods in a text written by a European.

THE MISSION TRAIL

Father Junípero Serra's grand design for Alta California nearly collapsed in the weeks that followed the expedition's return. Despite the friar's pleas, Portolá gave orders to prepare to march back to Loreto. Waiting too long to leave San Diego, the captain reasoned, would doom the entire expedition.

Everyone at the mission understood the reasons behind Portolá's decision. The long-awaited supply ship was overdue, and food stocks were running low. Water was scarce, and crops withered in the rocky soil. Even Father Serra had to admit that he was making little progress with the local American Indians, the Diegueños. At night the men of the tribe delighted in awakening the Spaniards with a chorus of bloodcurdling yells.[1] In the confusion, thieves darted into the mission to steal blankets from the beds. At first the guards fired their muskets into the air to frighten off the vandals. Only when they caught a band of Diegueños raiding the storehouse did they shoot to kill.

After Portolá set March 19, 1770, as the departure date, Serra and his fellow friars redoubled their prayers. Surely God would not forsake them! On March 18, as if in answer to their prayers, lookouts spotted a sail on the horizon. It was the *San Antonio*, loaded with a lifesaving cargo of rice, beans, and flour. As the tiny colony rejoiced, Portolá and Serra begin planning the return to Monterey.

Portolá Finishes His Task

Portolá saw his mission in military terms. A strong base at Monterey, he reasoned, would help Spain hold California against its European rivals. Now, with ample supplies on hand, he felt he was ready to finish the job. A few days after the captain led a small detachment up the coast, Serra sailed north in the *San Antonio*. Blessed by mild spring weather along El Camino Real, the land party reached the bay a week before the ship arrived. When the soldiers checked the large wooden cross they had raised near Carmel, they found piles of shellfish, feathers, and arrows at its base. The local villagers, noting the reverence the visitors had shown the cross, had added their own offerings.

On June 3, 1770, Father Serra marked their return by leading the company in prayers and hymns. Offshore, the *San Antonio* fired its cannon in counterpoint to the tolling of bells and volleys of musket fire. A friar placed a statue of the Virgin Mary on a makeshift altar. Serra sprinkled the ground with holy water. Then, as he noted in his diary, "[A]fter raising aloft the standard of the King of Heaven, we unfurled the flag of our Catholic Monarch likewise. As we

The soaring coast redwoods first described by Father Juan Crespi in 1769 are close cousins to the even taller giant sequoias. Early settlers logged these great trees and used the lumber to build forts. Here, Becky Green, the author's granddaughter, gazes up in awe at the sequoia that towers above her.

raised each one of them, we shouted at the top of our voices: 'Long live the Faith! Long live the King!'"[2]

Portolá stepped forward to claim the land in the name of Charles III. With the mission site properly blessed, the soldiers set to work. Within a month, they had erected a mission building and a small *presidio* (fort). His task finished, Portolá turned his command over to Pedros Fages and sailed for Mexico in the *San Antonio*. The report he sent to the viceroy from the coastal port of San Blas started bells ringing in Mexico City's church towers. The Spanish believed that Alta

California belonged to Spain, no matter what the Russians claimed. The Spanish forces, though, were spread terribly thin. In 1770, California's entire population of priests, friars, soldiers, and neophytes (native converts) numbered only sixty-three.

Coping with Adversity

Spain's first task was to tame the wilderness between San Diego and Monterey. With that goal in mind, the viceroy ordered the founding of five more missions along El Camino Real. A lesser man than Serra, who now reigned as Father-President of the missions, might have given up. Everywhere he turned, supplies and skilled labor were in short supply. To make matters worse, the Spanish government interfered with the work of the missions. Many of the rules were grounded in the fear of American Indian attacks. The friars, for example, were forbidden to leave the mission grounds without armed escorts.

For the first few years, supply lines were stretched to the breaking point. Some of the ships dispatched from Mexico were lost at sea. When a ship did make port, its cargo was never enough to meet the colony's needs. The caravans that traveled over El Camino Real faced similar hazards. After leaving the base at Loreto, pack trains had to cross hundreds of miles of barren wasteland. Father Serra argued that he needed 1,500 mules to supply Alta California's needs. In the 1770s, that was more mules than could be found in all of northern Mexico.[3] The supply problem did not ease until Juan Bautista de Anza blazed an overland route from New Mexico in 1774.

As supplies began to trickle in, Father Serra's friars labored to build a chain of missions. Only within mission walls, they believed, could converts be weaned from their old way of life. In addition to performing religious duties, the friars taught farming, weaving, carpentry, and stonework. At first, working with native labor, they pounded wood poles into the ground and roofed the walls with reeds. After 1785, as craftsmen arrived from Mexico, they began building with adobe bricks. Lacking heavy timbers to support the high tile roofs, the builders designed long, narrow sanctuaries. Workmen shaped the clay tiles over wooden molds before firing them.

Missions were designed as self-contained communities. Each was built in a hollow square, with the church anchoring the northeast corner. The other three sides provided sleeping rooms for unmarried women, housing for the friars, a barracks for soldiers, a large kitchen, and a series of workshops. Families lived nearby in clusters of thatched huts. Weavers, potters, leatherworkers, blacksmiths, and carpenters gathered at the mission workshops each day to practice their trades. As their skills increased, native craftsmen carved wood and stone to decorate the mission's arches and doorways. Nighttime activities were carried on in the light of flickering candles made of tallow, a hard fat taken from the carcasses of the mission livestock.

Missions were designed to be self-contained communities. Each was built as a hollow square, with the church in the northeast corner.

Forging Links in the Mission Chain

Father Serra's goal was to link Monterey and San Diego by opening missions a day's journey apart. In July 1771, he walked seventy-five miles south to the San Antonio River. After picking a likely site, he hung a wooden bell lined with metal on an oak tree. "Hear O Gentiles! Come! Come to the Holy Church of God! Come and receive the faith of Christ!" he called as he rang the bell. As often happened in the early years, no one answered the call. A single American Indian watched from a distance as Serra celebrated the first

Mass at the site.[4] Their religious duties done for the moment, the friars turned their cattle out to graze.

One by one, the Franciscans forged new links in the chain. Friars from San Diego plodded north along El Camino Real and founded the fourth mission at San Gabriel. Pack trains delivered food, seeds, and farm equipment. The mules also carried the tools of the priestly trade—chalices, statues, incense, and baptismal fonts. For the moment, the friars had few calls to perform baptisms. The American Indians kept their distance.

By the time he died in 1784, Father Serra had seen the birth of nine missions. Gain the people's trust, he told his friars, and you will be free to save souls. True to his orders, the friars learned to speak the local languages, treated the sick, and handed out food and clothing. If wild animals threatened a village, the missions sent soldiers to track them down. The soldiers, unfortunately, were far from home and poorly disciplined. In his diary Serra complained of the "bad soldier, who soon after arrival was caught in actual sin with an Indian woman."[5] American Indian women quickly learned to hide when Spanish horsemen rode toward their villages. To avenge injuries done to the women, their husbands and brothers ambushed pack trains and stole mission cattle.

In 1775 eight hundred Diegueños burned the San Diego mission. Spanish officials struck back by condemning four Diegueño leaders to death. Despite these troubles, California did not suffer a large-scale uprising like the revolt that hit New Mexico in 1680. For the most part, the growing mission system isolated the tribes and kept warriors from joining forces to start a rebellion. The American Indian population also fell as disease cut a deadly swath through the villages. At the presidios, the arrival of new settlers, especially young women, allowed the soldiers to hope for a normal family life.

San Francisco Solano, the last of the twenty-one missions, opened its doors in 1823. From Father Serra onward, the Franciscans had reached out to the California tribes with gifts of food, trinkets, clothing, and blankets. Those natives who joined the mission community agreed to follow a routine of work and worship. In return for their meals and training, the neophytes worked in the fields or in the mission workshops. The mission system was in full bloom—but criticism was growing. Once people were welcomed into the mission family, they were never allowed to leave. Soldiers pursued runaways and dragged them back. Serious offenses were punished by floggings.

End of an Era

At their height, the California missions ruled a vast empire. In 1832, the mission at San Luis Rey (forty miles north of San Diego) counted 2,788 neophytes in its annual tally. Those workers helped care for 27,500 cattle, 26,100 sheep, 1,300 goats, 300 pigs, 1,950 horses, and 180 mules.[6] The fertile fields and groves produced wheat, barley, corn, beans, olives, and oranges. At the close of the mission era in 1834, some thirty-one thousand neophytes were working on mission lands. This captive workforce carried out its tasks under the direction of sixty friars and three hundred soldiers.

As the 1800s dawned, the Spanish empire was crumbling. England and the Netherlands were challenging Spain for control of its overseas possessions. In the New World, Spanish colonies were struggling for independence. Mexican rebels began their revolution in 1810. By 1821 a newly formed Republic of Mexico

Spanish rancheros were vulnerable to American Indian attacks. In this 1886 engraving, Fredric Remington captured the moment when news arrived that Geronimo and his Apaches were on the warpath.

was setting its own course. A few years later, the order went out from Mexico City to secularize the missions. The Franciscans had long resisted this move, which meant that mission lands must be turned over to the American Indian workers. The neophytes, the friars believed, were ill prepared to manage their own affairs.

In 1830, in all of Alta California, less than thirty pieces of property were in private hands. All that changed in 1834 when the new decree took effect. Government officials allowed the church to keep only the land the mission buildings stood on. The rest of the acreage was divided into small farm plots and turned over to the mission workers. The concept of private ownership was foreign to most neophytes, however. Some simply walked away. Others sold out for a few gold coins or gambled their land away. To make matters worse, the death rate soared as epidemics swept through the villages. Within fifteen years, 90 percent of the newly freed American Indians would be dead.

★ A Day in the Life of a Mission ★

American Indians who heard the call of the missions exchanged their traditional tribal life for a more rigid schedule. Some neophytes tried the new ways for a while and then fled back to their villages. Except in those missions where friars abused their charges, most converts fell into a routine of regular meals, useful labor, and Christian worship.

A typical mission day began at sunrise with the ringing of the mission bells. The bells brought the native converts,

Mission San Juan Bautista looks much as it did during the late 1700s. In those days, the friars and American Indian converts worked and worshipped in these sturdy, white-washed buildings. The bronze bell over the entrance became a symbol of the missions and their role in building California.

soldiers, and friars streaming into the sanctuary to celebrate mass. After the service, the mission cooks served a breakfast of *atole* (a soup made of roasted barley). When breakfast was over, the people took up their daily tasks. In the workshops, American Indian workers made blankets, furniture, saddles, and other products. Out in the fields the growing corn needed weeding and there were cattle to brand. Children scared birds away from ripening fruit and prepared wool for spinning. With a feast day approaching, the men had orders to slaughter two fat cows for the barbecue. Little was wasted. The meat went to the mission kitchen, and the hide went to the tannery. The tallow was used to make candles.

At noon the Indian converts gathered for a nourishing dish of *pozole* (a thick vegetable-and-beef soup). After the meal and an hour's siesta, they returned to their tasks. Only during the sowing and harvest seasons did farmworkers stay in the fields until nightfall. Their chores finished, the people rested, played games, chatted, or left the mission to go hunting and fishing. A few met with the friars to pursue their religious studies and to learn Spanish. At sundown the bells rang again to call everyone together for evening prayers. Afterward, the group split up. Families returned to their homes, and unmarried women went to their sleeping rooms in the mission. Older women kept watch to make sure the girls did not slip out to meet their *novios* (boyfriends).

Historians still argue about the value of this way of life. One school of thought condemns the friars for working overtime to destroy a rich native culture. The missions' defenders point out that the Franciscans believed that they were bringing salvation to a heathen people. The native converts could be harshly disciplined, but priests found guilty of excessive cruelty were supposed to be dismissed from the order. One writer studied the system and concluded that by today's standards most jobs "would be classed as light labor."[7] The workweek seldom exceeded forty hours, and care was taken to protect workers from injury.

IN ORDER TO TRAVEL AND TRANSPORT GOODS FROM SAN DIEGO TO MONTEREY IT IS NECESSARY TO PASS TWENTY OR MORE INDIAN TOWNS EITHER DIRECTLY THROUGH THEM, . . . OR AT LEAST WITHIN SIGHT OF THEM . . . AND THERE ARE NUMEROUS CLIFFS, BLUFFS, AND DIFFICULT PASSAGES WHERE THE NATIVES MIGHT, . . . DISPUTE THE WAY AND EVEN PREVENT TRAVELERS FROM PASSING. INSTANCES OF THIS ARE NOT LACKING. FOR EXAMPLE, IN THE YEAR [1772] THEY THREW STONES AND DARTS AT ME WHEN I WAS GOING DOWN TO SAN DIEGO AT A PLACE WHICH WE CALL EL RINCON. . . . [A]ND WE FOUND OURSELVES IN SUCH STRAITS THAT IT WAS NECESSARY, . . . TO PUNISH THE BOLDNESS OF THE INSOLENT FELLOWS, KILLING ONE OR MORE OF THEM BUT LOSING NONE OF OUR MEN. . . . IT IS PLAIN TO SEE THAT THERE IS NO MEANS OF FORFENDING THESE INJURIES THAN TO ESTABLISH PRESIDIOS AND MISSIONS IN SUITABLE PLACES.

—CAPTAIN PEDRO FAGES, 1775[8]

California's American Indians welcomed the Spanish when they first arrived. That friendship soured when unruly soldiers and abusive friars began to mistreat tribal members. Although the California tribes were not warlike, their stubborn courage earned the respect of Pedro Fages and his fellow commanders. When he wrote this report, the mission chain was in its infancy. In 1775 only five missions stood ready to welcome travelers making the long journey along El Camino Real.

A NEW ERA DAWNS

During the early 1800s, the mission system looked as solid as the Rocky Mountains. The system crumbled, however, when the new Mexican government handed down its secularization decree in 1834. Stripped of workers as well as fields and pastures, the church could not maintain the fine adobe structures. To bring in a little cash, the friars rented the outbuildings for use as inns, shops, and stores. A farmer housed his pigs at San Fernando mission. Father Serra's chapel at San Juan Capistrano was used for storing hay. As the months passed the old buildings fell into disrepair. Roofs collapsed as timbers rotted, and adobe walls melted in the winter rains.

The final blow fell in 1846. To raise money to defend California against the oncoming emigrants from the United States, the governor put the missions up for sale. By 1848 all but the mission at Santa Barbara had passed into private hands. Soon vandals were stripping the tiles from ceiling vaults and carting off the heavy doors. Weeds choked the aqueducts and owls nested in silent bell towers.

The crumbling walls of Mission San Jaun Capistrano remind visitors that the great days of the missions ended in the mid-1800s. Earthquakes, fires, and vandals left their mark on the proud stone buildings.

The American Indians cut loose from the missions fared no better. A few managed to keep the land they were given, but most exchanged one master for another. Adrift in a strange new world, they were gathered in by Mexican landowners. Known as *rancheros*, the landowners fed and housed their American Indian servants and field hands, but seldom paid wages. Angered by mistreatment, some of the converts fought to reclaim a vanishing way of life. After fleeing to their native villages, the young men joined bands that preyed on cattle herds and lonely ranches. The raiders had horses now, but the rancheros had better mounts and more firepower. Aided by soldiers from the presidios, their *vaqueros* (cowboys) tracked down the marauders and burned their villages.

A New Role for El Camino Real

In the years before the Gold Rush, the trade that moved over El Camino Real tied the province together. Pack trains and wheeled carts crawled up and down the bumpy roadway. American Indian laborers smoothed the way into the missions by dragging logs over the entry roads. Couriers galloped their horses from mission to mission. If the message was urgent, a rider could make the trip from San Diego to Sonoma in three and a half days.[1]

In 1827, a Frenchman named Auguste Duhaut-Cilly dropped anchor at San Diego. The captain took a liking to the friendly Californios (Mexican settlers), but found life on El Camino Real a little raw for his tastes. Invited to dine at the mission, he found that the food was less than appetizing:

> And as Fray Vicente vainly urged me to eat, Fray Fernando exclaimed: "It . . . must be that the air at the mission is not kind to strangers: I never see one of them do honor to our table." And while saying these words, he was arranging a salad of cold mutton, with onions, pimento and oil from the mission, the odor of which was nauseating. And having no knife, he tore this meat with his fingers and even with his teeth, mixing the whole by handfuls in a nicked plate, where were still seen some remnants of the supper of the evening before.[2]

On a later visit Duhaut-Cilly joined some Californios who were riding north to Mission San Luis Rey. To avoid the heat of the day, the party set out at ten o'clock on a bright moonlit night. The men laughed and drank brandy as they made their way along El Camino Real. All went well until they reached the San Dieguito River, which was nearing flood stage. The Frenchman was ready to turn back, but the Californios "entered boldly . . . into this torrent, and under pain of remaining alone I followed them." The current nearly swept the riders out to sea before the horses found safe footing on the far shore.[3]

Over in New Mexico, merchants had little to laugh about as they headed south on the forty-day trek to Chihuahua. El Camino Real de Tierra Adentro had changed little in over two hundred years. La Jornada del Muerto still claimed its share of victims. With no inns or missions during the trip, travelers carried their own bread, dried beef, corn, and beans. The sheep that were not eaten along the way could be sold at the end of the journey. A lieutenant commanded the twenty soldiers who escorted the long line of wagons. In addition, each merchant carried a rifle—and knew how to use it. Horses that broke down were exchanged for fresh mounts at the next presidio.

Chihuahua had grown into a major trading center. New Mexico's merchants trekked south to sell wool, buffalo robes, deer hides, beaver and bear pelts, pine nuts, salt, brandy, and blankets. For the return trip, the merchants loaded their wagons with ironware, fabrics,

As trade and traffic increased along El Camino Real, packhorses and wooden carts gave way to covered wagons. In New Mexico, Northbound caravans hauled tools, cloth, and medicines to settlers. When the wagons turned south again, they carried heavy loads of wool, hides, salt, and brandy.

buttons, perfumes, boots, writing paper, and medicines. For well-to-do customers, they added books, chocolate, sugar, tobacco, and fine liquors. Because money was scarce, most deals depended on trade. In a typical exchange, one merchant traded thirty-two bottles of brandy for a large roll of cloth.[4]

Spain's colonial rulers guarded their trade monopoly by closing their ports and borders to foreign merchants. That policy was forgotten when Mexico gained its independence. In 1821 trader William

Becknell blazed the Santa Fe Trail and received a hero's welcome in New Mexico. The reports he carried back to Missouri set off a business boom. After reaching Santa Fe, the search for more customers led traders down El Camino Real de Tierra Adentro to Chihuahua. Business was brisk, for the wagonloads of low-priced American goods found a ready market along the fast-growing frontier.

In California, William Alden Gale rode down El Camino Real in the early 1800s and saw huge herds of cattle grazing in the fields. The hides and tallow they produced, he knew, would bring good prices in Boston and New York.[5] Spurred by Gale's reports, eastern merchants jumped into the California trade. Some of the products they shipped were badly needed—farm tools, silverware, cooking pots, and firearms. The most profitable items appealed to the rancheros' love of luxury. The owners of the brig (a two-masted sailing ship) *Sachem* quickly sold out their cargo of Chinese fireworks, music boxes, wind-up toys, ornate furniture, and flesh-colored silk.[6]

To pay for the gaudy toys, the rancheros slaughtered and skinned thousands of cattle. Wooden carts carried the green hides and leather bags of tallow to the beaches and ports. The Americans who waited there paid $1.50 per cowhide. Shipped home to Boston, each hide rewarded the traders with a profit of $2.50 to $3.50.[7]

An Avalanche of Americans

Year by year, more Americans made the long trek to California. Some arrived on ships after making the long voyage around South America. Others found their way to the Far West on overland trails. The California Trail led westward from Missouri. The Old Spanish Trail led travelers westward from Santa Fe. The influx of Americanos worried the rancheros. These brash newcomers talked as though they were destined to rule the land. Back east, the Texans were celebrating their hard-won independence. Would California be next?

In this crucial time Mexico sent General Manuel Micheltorena to defend the province. The rancheros sensed a kindred spirit in this tall, handsome general. He had a charming smile and he shared their love of fiestas. His first test came in 1842, when Commodore Thomas ap Catesby Jones raised the Stars and Stripes over Monterey. From his base in Los Angeles, Micheltorena ordered his northern commander to solve the problem. He was too far away, he said, to "fly to the aid of Monterey." For once, inaction won the day. Jones learned that his country was not at war with Mexico after all. He restored the Mexican flag and sailed south to express his regrets.

The war that Jones had counted on broke out four years later. In April 1846, intent on regaining control of Texas (which had joined the United States in 1845), Mexican troops crossed the Rio Grande. When they ran into the U.S. Army, the shooting started. By the

Wagon trains driven by settlers and goldseekers crowded the streets of western towns in the mid-1800s. In this period photo, teams of slow-footed oxen slow traffic to a crawl as they plod through Silver City, New Mexico.

time the news reached California, a ragtag band of American settlers had taken matters into their own hands. Alarmed by rumors that Mexican troops were coming to expel them, the men stormed into Sonoma and took over the town. On June 14 they raised a flag and grandly proclaimed the birth of the Republic of California. The flag, with its star and crudely drawn grizzly bear, gave the short-lived rebellion a name—the Bear Flag Revolt. With the flag waving in the breeze, the Bears helped themselves to the town's food and liquor supplies. Three weeks later, on July 7, Commodore John Sloat of the U.S. Navy added fuel to the fire by once again raising the Stars and Stripes over Monterey.

General José Castro turned to the Southern California rancheros for aid. The rancheros, however, had little love for a Mexican government that had long ignored them. Rather than risk the loss of their land, they allowed Commodore Robert Stockton to march his sailors into Los Angeles. Farther south, John C. Frémont landed in San Diego and took the town without firing a shot. The fighting might have ended there, but Stockton left Captain Archibald Gillespie in charge. Stung by Gillespie's harsh policies, the rancheros took up arms. The superb horsemen drove the Americans out of Los Angeles and defeated General Stephen Kearney at San Pasqual. In January 1847 Stockton hurried back from Monterey to face the Californios near San Gabriel. Stockton's sailors and Kearney's soldiers won the day by beating back the rancheros' last wild charge.

A similar story of conquest was being written in New Mexico. Before marching on to California, General Kearney occupied the province with scarcely a shot fired in anger. When the Americans entered Santa Fe, the people braced themselves for burning and looting. To their amazement, Kearney stepped forward to assure them that his troops came as friends and protectors. For their part, the soldiers were charmed by their first taste of Santa Fe's relaxed lifestyle. As one writer notes, "Santa Fe was a riot of violent color, the men in slit breeches with silver spurs and flaring capes, the girls barelegged and friendly, the town gay with fandangos."[8]

When he left for California, Kearney turned New Mexico over to two colonels, Alexander Doniphan and Sterling Price. Price soon had his hands full as a force of New Mexicans and American Indians rose in revolt. His men won a bloody victory at Taos pueblo, but not before the rebels had killed a number of Americans. One of the victims was the newly installed governor, Charles Bent.

While rebellion flared and died, Doniphan was marching his men south on El Camino Real de Tierra Adentro. The soldiers shivered in the winter wind as they crossed the Jornada del Muerto. Thirty miles north of El Paso they defeated a strong Mexican force. In the days that followed the weather turned bitter cold as the column trudged across one snake-infested stretch of desert after another. On February 28, after winning one final battle, the ragged troops ended their mission by capturing Chihuahua.

Like all travelers on El Camino Real de Tierra Adentro, the soldiers found ways to amuse themselves. At night they played cards, sang songs, wrestled, and told jokes. On rest days they raced horses and held jumping contests. If they were near a village, the Americans joined in the festivals. The high point came at the town of Tomé. The soldiers watched spellbound as the townsfolk celebrated a feast day with a three-hour barrage of skyrockets and fireballs.

On February 2, 1848, Mexico and the United States signed the Treaty of Guadalupe Hidalgo. Mexico received $15 million, but gave up its claims to a vast territory that included Texas, New Mexico, Arizona, and California. Four months later, James Marshall found gold in the American River. California and El Camino Real would never be the same.

★ Viva la Fiesta! Fun and Games in Old California ★

Many American visitors to California fell in love with the relaxed lifestyle of the rancheros. Others were quick to point out the failings of these wealthy landowners. On one point, however, both sides agreed: The rancheros knew how to have fun.

Auguste Duhaut-Cilly cheered the skillful riders who took part in a bullfight at a San Luis Rey fiesta in 1827. When the bull entered the arena, he wrote, the swiftest rider "seized it by the tail." Then, after spurring his horse, "he overthrew the bull, sending it rolling in the dust." At that point, instead of killing the bull, the riders sent the animal back to pasture. Lacking fine horses, the mission's American Indian converts played their own games. The favorite, Duhaut-Cilly noted, was a ball game much like modern field hockey.[9]

The Frenchman witnessed a supreme feat of horsemanship in the *carrera del gallo*. After workers buried a rooster up to its neck, the riders took their places some distance away. One by one, riding at full speed, they leaned out of their saddles and tried to grab the bird by the head. The first man to succeed then did his best to protect his prize from the grasp of his fellows. Riders who fell became "the butt for the laughter and jeers of their comrades and the fair spectators of this strife."[10]

The early Californios loved to stage colorful fiestas. In a display of horsemanship called carrera del gallo, *a vaquero leans far out of his saddle to pluck a half-buried rooster from the ground.*

Forty years later, after the collapse of the missions, a journalist noted changes in the fun and games. The fiesta at San Antonio de Pala, Benjamin Truman reported, "has degenerated into a mild revelry." Even as the friar led prayers at the little church, merrymakers crowded into an enclosure made of woven willow branches. A dance platform stood at the center, and booths lined the four sides. Truman saw a butcher's shop, food stalls, a basket shop, and booths devoted to gambling. In one, "six Mexicans are playing poker; the silver dollars are piled high, and each man has his bottle of wine." Farther on he spied a shuffleboard and more games of chance.

That night, when the band struck up "La Paloma," the music was "almost drowned by the shuffling feet of the dancers." Men lined up on one side, women on the other.

SEPTEMBER 20. PROCEEDING ON OUR JOURNEY, WE TRAVELED FIFTEEN MILES OVER A FLAT PLAIN, TIMBERED WITH GROVES AND PARKS OF EVERGREEN OAKS, AND COVERED WITH A GREAT VARIETY OF GRASSES, WILD OATS, AND MUSTARD. SO RANK IS THE GROWTH OF MUSTARD IN MANY PLACES THAT IT IS WITH DIFFICULTY THAT A HORSE CAN PENETRATE THROUGH IT. NUMEROUS BIRDS FLITTED FROM TREE TO TREE, MAKING THE GROVES MUSICAL WITH THEIR HARMONIOUS NOTES. THE BLACK-TAILED DEER BOUNDED FREQUENTLY ACROSS OUR PATH, AND THE LURKING AND STEALTHY *COYOTES* WERE CONTINUALLY IN VIEW. WE HALTED AT A SMALL CABIN, WITH A *CORRAL* NEAR IT, IN ORDER TO BREATHE OUR HORSES AND REFRESH OURSELVES. . . .

TWENTY-FIVE MILES, AT A RAPID GAIT OVER A LEVEL AND FERTILE PLAIN, BROUGHT US TO THE RANCHO OF DON FRANCISCO SANCHEZ, WHERE WE HALTED TO CHANGE HORSES. BREATHING OUR ANIMALS A SHORT TIME, WE RESUMED OUR JOURNEY AND REACHED THE MISSION OF SAN FRANCISCO DOLORES, THREE MILES FROM THE TOWN OF SAN FRANCISCO, JUST AFTER SUNSET. BETWEEN THE MISSION AND THE TOWN THE ROAD IS VERY SANDY, AND WE DETERMINED TO REMAIN HERE FOR THE NIGHT, CORRALLING THE LOOSE ANIMALS AND PICKETING THOSE WE RODE. . . . AFTER SEVERAL APPLICATIONS, WE WERE AT LAST ACCOMMODATED BY AN OLD AND VERY POOR CALIFORNIA SPANIARD, WHO INHABITATED A SMALL HOUSE IN ONE OF THE RUINOUS SQUARES. . . . ALL THAT HE HAD (AND IT WAS BUT LITTLE) WAS AT OUR DISPOSAL. A MORE MISERABLE SUPPER I NEVER SAT DOWN TO; BUT THE SPIRIT OF GENUINE HOSPITALITY IN WHICH IT WAS GIVEN IMPARTED TO THE POOR VIANDS A FLAVOR THAT RENDERED THE ENTERTAINMENT ALMOST SUMPTUOUS. . . .

—EDWIN BRYANT, 1846[11]

Edwin Bryant, an ailing journalist, traveled to California in 1846. As these passages suggest, he enjoyed his rides through the countryside. A few weeks later, Bryant found himself in the midst of the Bear Flag Revolt.

"There is no conversation, no small talk, flirtation, or coquetry beyond the speaking black eyes." In Truman's opinion, the best fun came when the young men smashed hollowed out eggs over the heads of their favorite girls. Each eggshell, he told his readers, released "a shower of gold and tinsel that glittered like diamonds in the candle light."[12]

Historian Thomas Chavez looks at the history of the Southwest and shakes his head in wonder. He sees a culture that somehow mixed American Indians, Hispanics, and Anglos in "a shotgun marriage that worked out." As in most marriages, Chavez says, the partners had to learn to live with each other.

"A FRENZY SEIZED MY SOUL"

First the Spanish moved in and took much of the best land from the American Indians. Then Mexico threw off the Spanish yoke, only to lose the immense region to the onrushing Americans.[1]

Ever since the 1820s, settlers had trickled into California. More might have come west, but the long trek across prairies and mountains was a daunting prospect. After the winter of 1846, the story of the luckless Donner party added to the fears. Trapped high in the Sierras by deep snow, the survivors saved themselves by eating human flesh. Then came the news that gold had been found at Sutter's Mill. Slowly at first, and then in a mighty torrent, gold seekers hurried west to "strike it rich."

Coastal towns nearly emptied as the fever spread

during the summer of 1848. Workmen laid down their tools, soldiers fled their posts, and husbands left their families. Newspapers shut down and San Francisco harbor was clogged with ships whose crews had deserted. A jailer in San Jose took his prisoners with him when he ran off to make his fortune. James Carson imagined piles of gold filling his path and beautiful women chasing him. This violent attack of gold fever, he said, was "a frenzy [that] seized my soul."[2]

New Jobs for Old Roads

With the flag of the United States flying over New Mexico, traffic on El Camino Real de Tierra Adentro grew lighter. Some goods bound for Mexico moved through Santa Fe, but eastern merchants preferred the shorter route through Texas. The locals still favored the old road, however, and stagecoach lines made regular runs between Santa Fe and El Paso.

Traveling south to Chihuahua with her trader husband in 1846, newcomer Susan Magoffin saw some amazing sights. New Mexican women, the young Easterner noted, pulled their skirts up over their knees while wading across a creek. Even stranger was the sight of women smoking, gambling, and shopping on the Sabbath. "It is truly shocking," she noted in her diary.[3] Later, as she made friends and learned more about Mexican culture, she softened her views.

The heaviest traffic through New Mexico after 1848 was headed west, not south. Once the gold-seeking

The California Gold Rush drew adventurers from around the globe. Panning for golden flakes in rivers meant long days of backbreaking labor. A lucky few struck it rich, but most found barely enough gold to pay their expenses.

Forty-Niners reached San Diego, they turned north on California's El Camino Real. Other gold seekers arrived by ship at San Francisco, and a third group trudged overland on the California Trail. Few stopped to wonder at the sad state of the once-proud missions. Richard Henry Dana, Jr., returned after a twenty-four-year absence to find the San Diego Mission "gone to decay. The buildings are unused and ruinous, and the large gardens show now only wild cactuses, willows, and a few olive trees."[4] Don Santiago Arguello now owned the mission's fifty-eight thousand acres. Governor Pio Pico had given the land to rancher in return for a promise to pay the mission's debts.

As the Gold Rush picked up speed in 1849, men from all walks of life hurried to claim their share. In those early days, with gold selling for $16 an ounce, a handful of men became wealthy overnight. Four Mormons showed up in Los Angeles with a hundred pounds of pure gold. A German merchant bought an eighty-ounce nugget from an American Indian chief—and paid for it with cheap trinkets. A Los Angeles man picked a spot near Sonora and started digging. Three feet down he struck a vein that yielded fifty-two pounds of gold. By contrast, the average miner was lucky to find an ounce or two a day. All too soon, the easy veins played out. Most of the gold-seekers who swarmed over the gold fields went broke.

As prices soared, a new business emerged: "mine the miners." Merchants paid $500 a month for the new wooden buildings that sprang up along El Camino Real. They knew that miners heading out to the gold fields would pay almost any price. One shopkeeper marked all of his shovels, boots, tin pans, and gallon jugs of whiskey with the same price: $100. The rancheros jumped into the game as well. The trade in hides had collapsed, but a six-dollar horse now sold for $300. Hungry miners paid $3 per egg and $6 a pound for butter.[5] A few of the newcomers, penniless and desperate, stripped orchards and looted barns.

By the mid-1850s the rancheros were facing a far graver threat. Rustlers stole their cattle, and squatters camped on their land. When they rode into town, crooked gamblers cheated them at the card tables. The final blow was delivered by the laws of the new state. Judges conspired with greedy politicians and crooked lawyers to reject vaguely written Spanish land grants. Their unjust verdicts left squatters and land sharks free to subdivide and sell the once-prosperous ranchos. The cities of Oakland and Berkeley took root on land that once belonged to the immense Peralta rancho.[6]

Perils of the Open Road

Outlaws thrived in the winner-take-all atmosphere of the Gold Rush. Even when lawmen managed to clean up a town, they could do little to keep the roads safe. Elizabeth Farnham thought the problem started with children who ran loose in the mining towns. "I saw boys, from six upwards, swaggering through the streets," she wrote. The young toughs dressed in scarlet sashes, smoked cigars, and uttered "huge oaths."[7] Scarred by neglect, some of these boys quite likely grew up to become bandits, rustlers, and highwaymen.

The most famous of California's colorful outlaws was the legendary Joaquin Murrieta. Legend says that Joaquin turned to crime after he saw his brother killed by white miners. Because he mostly targeted Americans, the Californios adopted him as a folk hero. Even his foes agreed that Murrieta was a genius with horses, guns, knives, and the lasso. In the early days, he waylaid lone travelers and slit their throats. As his fame spread, he attracted followers like Vicente Chavez. The sadistic Chavez liked to torture his captives by sewing them into wet cowhides. Then he laughed with delight as the drying hides shrank and slowly strangled his victims. The bloodthirsty Three-Fingered Jack also killed his victims slowly. He once remarked, "Brandy makes some men drunk, but give me blood."[8]

In 1853 the state dispatched a squad of rangers to wipe out Joaquin and his gang. Warned of the danger, Joaquin headed south. Along the way he left a trail of burning ranches. Then, instead of continuing to Baja, he doubled back and rode north through the San Joaquin Valley. His luck ran out when the rangers stumbled on his camp early one morning. The blazing

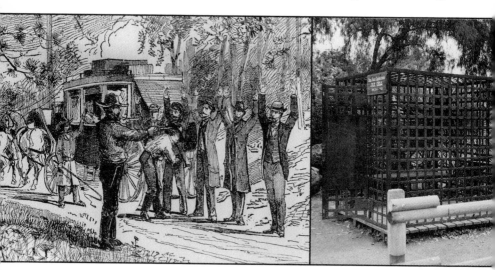

Stagecoach passengers were a favorite target of outlaw gangs. Robbers who were unlucky enough to get caught could expect to spend time in iron-barred jail cells if they escaped being hung from a nearby tree.

gunfight that followed ended with the death of Joaquin and three gang members. To prove that the outlaws really were dead, the rangers cut off Joaquin's head and Three-Fingered Jack's hand. At a nearby army post a doctor preserved the head and the hand in alcohol. Before long the people of San Francisco were lining up to pay a dollar apiece to view Joaquin's head.[9]

Traveling El Camino Real

In the 1850s, gold seekers who had traveled the well-paved National Road from Maryland to Illinois laughed at El Camino Real. "Do you call that a road?" they sneered when they saw California's main north-south route. The forty-foot wide wood-planked toll road that led out of San Francisco ended at Sixteenth Street. From there the roadbed was smooth until the road reached the Red House Inn a few miles farther on. Travelers bound for Los Angeles stopped at the inn for "bird, chicken and wine breakfasts, served at all hours of the day and night."[10] Ahead lay four hundred miles of hard going.

Like many of the nation's roads, El Camino Real tested the pioneer spirit. The route skirted ocean cliffs, climbed through rocky passes, and crossed brush-covered wilderness. Travelers splashed across streams, waited for flooded rivers to fall, and huddled together at night around small campfires. The towns they passed through welcomed them with food, lodging, and amusements. Santa Barbara's main street was crowded with saloons and gambling halls. South of the town a long stretch of seaside road vanished each day when the tide rolled in.[11]

Journalist Edwin Bryant kept a detailed account of his travels in California. He was especially impressed by the two men who galloped the length of El Camino Real in just three days. The trick, he noted, was to travel with at least ten horses and a vaquero to tend them. After a twenty-mile run, each rider picked a fresh horse from the pack. As these mounts tired, the riders switched again. If a horse showed signs of wearing out, the vaquero turned it loose. "Horseflesh is cheap," Bryant explained, "and the animal must go as long as he can. And when he cannot travel longer he is left, and another horse is substituted."[12]

Stagecoach Lines Usher in a New Age

The demand for faster mail delivery led to long distance express services. One early effort was known as the Jackass Mail. The line's hard-working mules hauled letters and packages from San Antonio to San Diego in three to four weeks. In 1858, John Butterfield's Overland Mail, aided by a $600,000 federal contract, took up the challenge. A skeptical public scoffed at the plan to deliver mail coast-to-coast in only twenty-five days. The first westbound stage followed a route that led to San Francisco by way of El Paso and Los Angeles. Instead of hugging the coast above Los Angeles, the stage veered inland and clattered up the San Joaquin Valley. Relay stations furnished the fresh horses that

San Francisco's civic leaders crowd aboard an Overland Mail stagecoach for a ceremonial ride. When the coach leaves for its five or six day run down El Camino Real it will be carrying five passengers and their baggage.

kept the stage rolling at a splendid fifteen miles an hour. The stage cut back to El Camino Real over Pacheco Pass, sped through San Jose, and on to San Francisco. A cheering crowd greeted the final driver when he pulled up in front of the Overland Mail office. Total travel time: twenty-three days, twenty-three hours, and thirty minutes.[13]

The army imported camels to transport supplies across the desert in the 1860s. Although the "ships of the desert" displayed speed and endurance, the trial did not go well. The camels' rolling gait make their riders seasick, and their smell panicked livestock. After a few trips, the army gave up and sold the animals at auction. The camels then vanished from view, although "wild camel sightings" surfaced well into the 1900s.[14] The only surviving physical proof that wild camels once roamed the Southwest is a camel skeleton stored at the Smithsonian in Washington, D.C.

During the 1860s the U.S. Army imported camels to carry supplies across the deserts. When the camels proved hard to manage, the army abandoned the experiment. Some of the animals ended up in circuses—but wild herds survived well into the 1900s.

By this time local stage lines were running between the larger towns. One stagecoach line rattled the fifty miles from San Francisco to San Jose in nine hours. The coaches carried eight to ten passengers, who paid $32 one way (or two ounces of gold). If the stage bogged down in the mud, the passengers were told to get out and push. One of the more colorful drivers was tobacco-chewing, hard-cussing "Cockeyed" Charley Parkhurst. Some said Charley, who wore a patch over one eye, was the best and fastest of them all. When his reflexes slowed down, Charley climbed down from the driver's seat and opened a bar. He died in 1879—and only then did the startling news come out. Charley Parkhurst was really a woman! Charlotte Parkhurst had kept her secret well, and had even voted in the 1868 election. The rest of the nation's women did not gain the vote for another fifty-three years.[15]

Even before Charley died, a new age was dawning. In 1860 Pony Express riders stole business from the stage lines by carrying mail from Missouri to Sacramento in just ten days. Sixteen months later, the first east-west telegraph line put the Pony Express out of business. In a similar fashion, traffic on El Camino Real dropped sharply after rail service linked the state's cities in 1864. A harder blow fell in 1869, when the transcontinental railroad carried its first passengers. For the next forty years, the iron horse reigned as king of long-distance travel.

★ BLACK BART: LEGENDARY HIGHWAYMAN ★

The command was always the same: "Throw down the box!" And twenty-seven times, between 1875 and 1883, Wells Fargo stage drivers did as they were told. Rather than defy the man holding the shotgun, they tossed down the express boxes. The daring robberies introduced California to the highwayman known as Black Bart.

Bart worked alone, was never seen on a horse, and wore a flour sack over his head. He never fired his double-barreled shotgun, and he refused to steal from women. Most notably, he scribbled poems and left them behind after some of his holdups. His verse helped make the outlaw poet (spelled "Po8") famous:

> *here I lay me down to sleep*
> *to wait the coming morrow*
> *perhaps success perhaps defeat*
> *and everlasting Sorrow*
> *let come what will I'll try it on*
> *My condition can't be worse*
> *and if theres money in that box*
> *Tis munny in my purse*

—Black Bart, the Po8[16]

Lawmen combed the hills, but Bart always slipped away. Large rewards were posted, but no one claimed the money. A woman who saw Bart while he was fleeing the scene of a holdup remembered his gray hair and fine mustache. "He looked like a preacher," she said.[17]

Bart's twenty-eighth robbery was also his last. He stopped a coach near the top of a hill, only to find the express box bolted to the floor. Keeping the driver covered, Bart set to work to pry the box loose. He did not know that a passenger had left the coach at the bottom of the hill to do some hunting. Just as Bart finished with the box, the man caught up with the stage. Seeing Bart backing away from the stage, moneybags in hand, the hunter opened fire. The first hurried shots missed. A second volley winged Bart as he ran through the brush, but he kept going. A later search of the hillside turned up only a derby, a razor, and a bloody handkerchief.[18]

Good detective work traced the handkerchief to a San Francisco laundry. The owner recognized the laundry mark and led investigators to fifty-five-year-old Charles Bolton. When they picked him up, the well-dressed "mining engineer" protested, "I am a gentleman."[19] Further questioning led to a full confession. Bolton's real name was Charles Boles. After serving in the Civil War, he had left his family to seek his fortune out west. Although he lived well on his loot, Boles was no spendthrift. After his arrest he returned a big chunk of the $18,000 he had stolen.

Boles earned a parole after serving four years in San Quentin, a prison near San Francisco. When reporters asked him if Black Bart was about to resume his old trade, Boles shook his head. "Young man, didn't you just hear me say I will commit no more crimes?" he snapped.[20]

After that, Boles vanished from view. Some say he died in New York City in 1917. Others like to believe that he headed off to Montana for another try at striking it rich.

WHEREAS THE COACH CONTAINING THE U.S. MAILS AND EXPRESS WAS ON THE 18TH ROBBED NEAR ALAMILLO (ON THE CAMINO REAL) IN SOCORRO COUNTY AND WHEREAS IT IS KNOWN THAT THREE PERSONS WERE ENGAGED IN THE SAID ROBBERY WHO ARE BELIEVED TO BE DESPERATE MEN. NOW THEREFORE, I, G. B. AXTELL, GOV. OF SAID TERRITORY DO HEREBY OFFER A REWARD OF $500.00 FOR THE APPREHENSION OF SAID MEN TO BE TAKEN ALIVE IF POSSIBLE.

NEW MEXICO, APRIL 30, 1877[21]

Beginning in 1783 the governor of New Mexico established a regular mail delivery between Santa Fe and El Paso. By 1815 the postal service kept a monthly schedule along El Camino Real de Tierra Adentro. After the Mexican War, the first stagecoach lines appeared and offered both mail and passenger service. This reward notice reminds us that stagecoach passengers faced hazards far more threatening than hard seats, bumpy roads, and desert heat.

Living "out west" seemed to inspire people to grand deeds and grander claims. Westerners said their land was bigger, richer, and more beautiful than any other on earth. A guidebook of the day promised that California's climate was healthful, its soil productive, and the scenery beyond compare. The

FROM GOLD RUSH TO LAND BOOM

customs might be strange to newcomers, the author noted, but they were lawful and civilized. After getting an earful of this boasting, a visitor snorted, "In California every bush is a tree, every hill a mountain, and every man a damned liar."[1]

Until the 1860s and 1870s, time and distance combined to limit growth in the West. Whether newcomers came overland or by sea, the journey was long and dangerous. Then, almost overnight, the railroads changed all that.

Progress Moves on Iron Rails

The railroads came to New Mexico and California within the same ten-year period. The Royal Highways had performed well, but people were weary of travel

The coming of the railroads ended the era of travel by covered wagon over unpaved roads such as El Camino Real. On the train, the journey westward was bumpy, but fares were cheap.

by horse and mule. Everyone longed for the speed of travel by rail. The April 1859 issue of *Hutchings' California Magazine* made the point quite clearly:

> Now for ourselves we want to see this "iron horse" snorting and puffing through one of the many passes of the Sierra Nevada mountains. And as he rushes on, on, beneath the shadows of our densely timbered forests, or darts across or down our beautiful and fertile valleys, we don't care if all the Indians in creation lift up their hands in wonder at it, . . . We want a Railroad.
>
> What care we if this or that political party . . . jump astride it, and seek to ride into power upon it. All we

say is—*give us the Railroad,* give it to us *somebody*—give it to us *anybody*—give it to us *everybody.* It is the RAILROAD that we want; and we will not quarrel about the source from whence it comes. . . . *Progress* prays for it [and] *Commerce* waits for it.[2]

For all its golden promise, California was sinking into an economic swamp. Most of the state's half million people lived near dusty old El Camino Real. Now that the gold fields were mostly played out, they worked for low wages—if they had jobs. Farmers and ranchers also felt the pinch. They begged for a faster, cheaper way to ship their products to market.

Just as the need was greatest, a railroad boom sent shining tracks snaking across the land. The Union Pacific (UP) earned bragging rights by running the first trains west over the transcontinental railroad in 1869. The UP's rivals were not far behind. Helped by generous land grants, the Southern Pacific (SP) connected Los Angeles with New Orleans in 1881. Four years later the Atchison, Topeka and Santa Fe Railroad opened its Chicago to Los Angeles route. The SP, hoping to crush the competition, promptly cut its $125 fare in half. The Santa Fe hit back by slashing its own fares. By the winter of 1886 people were traveling from Kansas City or New Orleans for $25 dollars. From there the price fell to $12, then to $8.

In March 1887 the Santa Fe played its last card. The line's ads trumpeted, "Kansas City to Los Angeles—*One Dollar!*" Once again, to the delight of west-bound travelers, the SP matched the giveaway fare.³ People flooded into California, and many stayed, reluctant to pay the $100-plus return fare. Towns along El Camino Real grew like wildfire. In seven years, San Diego's population jumped sixfold, from 8,700 to fifty thousand.

In New Mexico, the Atchison, Topeka and Santa Fe railroad ran its first trains in 1880. The people were demanding rail service, and the owners wanted to keep the Southern Pacific out of the region. As Southern Pacific's crews built east from Los Angeles, the Santa Fe pushed a second line down from Colorado. The opening of service to the city of Santa Fe in February 1880 put an end to the great days of the Santa Fe Trail. Instead of jolting west in covered wagons, settlers and traders rode the rails in comfort. Building south along El Camino Real led straight into the Jornada del Muerto. To supply water to the thirsty steam locomotives, crews hurried to dig a series of deep wells. El Paso welcomed its first train on the new branch line in July 1881.

Mexico built its own line north from Chihuahua. The joining of the two lines at El Paso cut traffic on El Camino Real, but no one mourned. People were busy crossing the Rio Grande on a fine new bridge. The region welcomed an upsurge in cross-border trade, mostly in timber, coal, and lead and silver ore. The access to new markets also led to an upswing in ranching. In ten years, the number of cattle grazing in New Mexico grew from 347,000 to 1,630,000.⁴

Anxious to fill empty seats, the railroads cut fares and promoted California's warm sun and fertile soil. Later, the Southern Pacific switched to ads that promoted the states' scenic wonders, such as Yosemite National Park.

"It's a Big, Big BOOM!"

Ever since the 1840s, Horace Greeley of the *New York Tribune* had been urging his readers, "Go west, young man." Now, hard on the heels of the Gold Rush came a new wave of fortune-seekers. This time the lure was California land. Salesmen showered new arrivals with leaflets as they stepped off the trains. One handbill advised, "Come to glorious Santa Ana. Beautiful! Busy! Bustling! Bountiful! Booming!" The real come-on followed: "It's a big, big BOOM! And you CAN ACCUMULATE DUCATS [make money] BY INVESTING! SEE IT! SEE IT! SEE IT!"[5]

Along El Camino Real, land that once was a tough sell at $5 an acre now sold for five hundred times that price. The trick lay in picking a "hot" location. When a new town took root nearby, profits went through the roof. A smart buyer could purchase an acre for $3,000, cut it into six town lots—and sell each one for $2,500. As the fever grew, buyers rushed to be first in line when new subdivisions were about to open. Latecomers sometimes paid as much as $1,000 for a place near the head of the line.[6]

The lure of easy money attracted a small army of con artists. One man sold worthless lots in the Mojave Desert for $250 each. That was nearly all profit, because the lots cost only fifteen cents each. The boldest swindler of the day sold "groves" of California's "native orange trees" at $500 an acre. To those who argued that the orange tree was a Spanish import, he said, "Come and see." And sure enough, out in the desert, eager buyers saw oranges "growing" on gray and prickly Joshua trees. The swindler vanished before his customers learned that he had tied the oranges to the Joshua trees.[7]

After two frantic years, the land boom ran its course. In its wake, agriculture and tourism emerged to support California's economy. Farmers, many of whom were Chinese and Japanese immigrants, raised large crops of oranges, grapefruit, lemons, grapes, cherries, avocados, dates, and cotton. Oranges were the favorite cash crop. Washington navel oranges ripened in winter, Valencias during the summer. Growers hurried to meet the demand by planting more and more acres of orange groves.

The second bumper crop was tourism. Visitors splashed in the Pacific and gazed up at giant redwoods. They hiked the Yosemite Valley and visited ghost towns left in the wake of the Gold Rush. Easterners basked in the sun and marveled at the sight of strawberries ripening in February. When they tired of the outdoor life, they booked rooms at grand hotels or "took the cure" at a hot springs resort. John D. Rockefeller, one of the world's richest men, fell in love with the Santa Clara Valley. The valley, he said, was "a picture such as I have never seen. Why! it is even worth the expense of a trip across the continent."[8]

The Auto Brings New Life to El Camino Real

Men on foot and men riding horses and mules helped blaze the routes of the Royal Highways. Next came wooden-wheeled carts, followed by canvas-topped wagons. As the years passed, swift stagecoaches shoved the lumbering wagons aside. In the mid-1860s, rail travel emerged as the people's choice. Then, toward the end of the century, Americans wheeled out their "safety bicycles." Because they featured coaster brakes and wheels of equal size, the new bicycles were far less

Los Angeles paid a high price for its rapid development brought on by the land boom. In 1886, people were unprepared and without a drainage system when two days of heavy rain flooded the streets and sent residents on a frantic search for higher ground.

likely to tip over. Reckless cyclists took to the streets, leaving cursing wagon drivers and panicky horses in their wake. The police hit back by forming their own cycle squads. Bystanders agreed that a policeman "pedaling furiously after a 'scorcher [speeder],' his handle-bar mustache stiff in the breeze, was a thrilling sight."[9]

Fast or slow, cyclists longed for smooth, safe roads. The League of American Wheelman begged the federal government to do something. In 1893, Congress voted to spend $10,000 to look into the problem. The timing was good, for a far greater force for change was about to enter the scene. Frank Duryea showed off his first gasoline-powered horseless carriage in 1892. Two years later he thrilled spectators by averaging 5.25 miles per hour on a snowy racetrack. Out in California, a commission supported the building of twenty-eight state highways. The plan called for El Camino Real to serve as the backbone of the network.

The people who lived along the nation's roads jeered the arrival of the first automobiles. Who could afford this rich man's toy? The jeers changed to cheers in 1908 when Henry Ford's mass-produced Model T hit the market. Thanks to the low price tag, workers could motor to their jobs. Farmers could truck their produce to market. Families could go for Sunday drives in the country. The swift increase in auto traffic soon outpaced the efforts of road builders. In 1909, motorists who ventured out on El Camino Real jounced and scraped over a rutted dirt roadbed. Only a few miles were paved with asphalt. Farmers made good money by dragging "them rich city automobilists" out of mud holes. Drivers accused their rescuers of returning at night to refill the holes with water.[10]

In California, the state proposed an $18 million bond issue. The goal, which voters quickly approved, was to "motorize" El Camino Real. Road crews were soon laying smooth ribbons of concrete and asphalt. The major north-south route was named U.S. Highway 101 in 1926. For the most part, 101

Soon after Ford's Model T hit the road in 1908, motorists were bouncing over the rocks and ruts of El Camino Real. The growing demand for paved highways forced the states to begin paving the old mission roads.

followed the path first blazed by Juan de Portolá in 1769. At Rincón Point, where stages had once splashed through the surf, workers built a log overpass. One bond issue followed another as more drivers discovered the joys of motoring.

As auto traffic increased, California redoubled its efforts at road building. To make sure that El Camino Real would not be forgotten, in 1906 the Mission Bell Association put up 450 bronze bells along the old route. Spaced one mile apart, the bells hung from iron posts shaped like Franciscan walking staffs. At Mission San Francisco de Asis, California Historical Landmark No. 784 honors the birth of Father Junípero Serra. The plaque marks "the northern terminus [endpoint] of El Camino Real as Padre Serra knew it and helped to blaze it."

★ A GHOST STORY ★

In the 1870s, Benjamin Truman entertained newspaper readers with travel stories about the California missions. He was especially fond of the mission at San Juan Capistrano, a day's journey south of Los Angeles. "The traveler," he wrote, "may feast his eyes upon the solemn grandeur of the Pacific, upon the ruggedest of mountains . . . and upon streams . . . lined with wild poppies and daisies and lilies."[11]

During his visit, Truman watched workmen dig a hole big enough to hold a two-story house. The diggers explained that they were on the trail of pirate treasure that dated back to 1818. The hunters missed out on the gold and jewels, but the locals have unearthed a different kind of riches. San Juan Capistrano, they say, is host to a lively collection of ghosts.

One sad and lonely ghost is said to be the spirit of the beautiful Magdalena. The young American Indian girl loved the handsome Teofilo, but the two were forbidden to meet. Despite the order, the lovers often met secretly in the mission gardens. One day a friar caught them there, and ordered Magdalena to pray for forgiveness. On December 8, 1812, she walked into the mission church, carrying her penitent's candle. Just as she lit the candle, the earth began to shake. The floor pitched and rolled, and then the dome of the church collapsed. Rescuers dug out the bodies of forty people, including Magdalena. Now, at night, when visitors walk past the great church, they sometimes claim to see an eerie sight. High above them, lit by a flickering candle, floats the pale, solemn face of a young girl. Magdalena, the story assures us, is still doing penance for her forbidden love.[12]

The sight of Magdalena's ghost leaves viewers feeling sad, not frightened. Another ghost, La Llorona (the Weeping Woman), inspires a real sense of fear. Her ghost, the story says, haunts the banks of Trabuco Creek. At night passersby can hear her sobs and cries blending with the wind as it rushes along the tree-lined creek. Those who have heard the ghost keep their children safe at home on the nights La Llorona walks. They say she once drowned her own children in the dark, swirling waters of the creek. Now she is destined to walk the banks of the river forever, grieving for the innocents she murdered.[13] Keep your distance, the locals warn, or you may suffer the same fate as La Llorona's long-dead children!

A MOTORIST'S LOG, 1906

APRIL 14—NORDHOFF TO SANTA BARBARA: CROSSED NINE FORDS ON THE CREEK ROAD AND THREE STREAMS IN VENTURA RIVER. STUCK IN THIRD. YOUNG MAN WITH TEAM PULLED US OUT. LEFT THE ROAD AND RAN THROUGH FIELDS DOWN A VERY STEEP HILL BACK ONTO MAIN ROAD. OILED ROAD HORRIBLY ROUGH.

APRIL 24—WAITED AT SANTA BARBARA EIGHT DAYS FOR NEW TIRES FROM DENVER. PUT ON NEW TIRES AND WENT FOR RIDE. WATER PUMP GAVE OUT. BATTERY REPAIR WAS ALSO NECESSARY.

APRIL 25—SANTA BARBARA TO LOS OLIVOS: HAD TO STOP AT CREEK AND FILL RADIATOR. PIPE WORKING LOOSE ON TOP OF CYLINDERS. ROAD FROM HERE TO GAVIOTA HORRIBLE. CROSSED 45 CREEKS AND CANYONS UP ONE STEEP HILL AFTER ANOTHER. MOST DISCOURAGING. AT LAS CRUCES PASSED AUTOMOBILE WITH BROKEN SPRING. AFTER PASSING SANTA YNEZ MISSION ENGINE MISSING. TOOK OUT BATTERY AND PUT IN DRY CELLS. FILLED RADIATOR WITH TUMBLER FROM HORSE DRAUGHT.

APRIL 26—LOS OLIVOS TO SAN LUIS OBISPO. HIGH WIND BLOWING. STOPPED EVERY FEW MINUTES TO TIGHTEN UP WATER PIPE, OR FUSS WITH WIRING. SAND DEEP. MORE BATTERY TROUBLE. BROKE FRONT SPRING CLEAR IN TWO.

APRIL 27—SAN LUIS OBISPO: I DECIDED TO ABANDON CAR HERE.

—C. D. COX[14]

Anyone who has suffered car trouble will sympathize with the plight of C. D. Cox. The breakdown-prone automobiles of 1906 were no match for the rigors of El Camino Real.

8

SEARCHING FOR EL CAMINO REAL

Douglas and Christine Preston plunged deep into La Jornada del Muerto during their search for New Mexico's Royal Highway. The wilderness worked its magic one night while they were camped at Laguna del Muerto. As the Prestons sat around their small fire, the past seemed very close at hand.

We could almost imagine the wagons drawn into formation, hear the braying of mules and the clatter of harquebuses [muskets], and smell the smoke of innumerable cooking fires. . . . As night fell, the only sound was the wind shaking last year's dead rattleweed on the lake bottom. But then, carried on the still darkness of the desert night, we heard the sad whistle of the train—the death knell of the Camino Real.[1]

The trail is gone, but its influence remains. Even when the two nations disagree, the United States and Mexico are tied together by those long ribbons of road. Right from the start, Hispanic Americans helped mold our nation's culture. Even more, El Camino Real "is a symbol of the eternal human desire to explore, to move, to discover and settle new lands."[2]

The Past Is Not Totally Lost

Unlike the Prestons, most tourists have only a few days to devote to their quest for El Camino Real. Even so, all is not lost. In New Mexico, surveys show that at least one-third of the old trail from El Paso north to San Juan remains. Observers can spot the faint ruts and changes in plant growth that date back to the 1600s. Visitors, however, want to see more than wheel ruts.

Most of today's drivers speed through the country-side without realizing that they are retracing routes blazed by early explorers. In New Mexico, U.S.

El Camino Real still plays an important role in the lives of people living in remote Mexican villages. Like the wagoneers of old, bus drivers have no choice but to splash across flooded streambeds.

Highway 25 carries traffic along much of the old El Camino Real de Tierra Adentro. In California, U.S. Highway 101 follows the route of Father Serra's original Royal Highway. On either route, drivers easily cover two hundred miles by lunchtime. In the 1850s, that same two hundred miles would have taken from two to fourteen long, hard days. A traveler's speed depended on the method of travel:

> Wagon train—fourteen days (15 miles per day)
> On foot—six days (36 miles per day)
> Horseback—three days (70 miles per day)
> Stagecoach—two days (110 miles per day)[3]

Brian Wood and Matt Labovitz hopped on their bicycles when they set out to retrace the mission highway for California Missions Interactive. As a guide, they followed a journal kept by a man who visited the missions on muleback in 1856. They found the route much changed—not always for the better. At one point the bike path led them onto Highway 101. The five-mile stretch ran close to the ocean, but they could not pause to enjoy the view. "Too many large cars and trucks whizzing by!" they reported. "Our journey definitely wasn't as peaceful (or as safe) as Mr. Miller's."[4]

Searching For the Past: New Mexico

Although the adventurous tour El Camino Real by bicycle, most tourists are content to travel by car. The real test is to seek out the locations along U.S. 25 that give the best insights into the region's history. Visitors with a good guidebook can explore any period of the state's history that interests them. Here are some good places to start:

Santa Fe Plaza

The open square that lies at the center of New Mexico's capital delights the heart as well as the senses. Until 1880, the Santa Fe Trail ended here. For southbound traders, El Camino Real began here. Fine shops and restaurants line three sides, but the real treasure lies on the north side. The Palace of the Governors is a rambling adobe that has been in use since 1610. Over the years it has served as the headquarters of Spanish, Mexican, and United States governors. Today it houses the Museum of New Mexico. The museum's colorful exhibits trace the state's story from prehistory to the present.

Santa Fe's Churches

From the Plaza, a walk in almost any direction takes a visitor to fine old adobes, museums, art galleries, and churches. One route follows the Old Santa Fe Trail to the Loretto Chapel. Back in 1878, when the chapel was new, the nuns found that builders had not constructed a stairway to the choir loft. As if in answer to their prayers, a carpenter appeared and set to work. He vanished after the job was done, leaving behind a "miracle staircase" built without nails or visible supports. A few more steps take visitors to the Chapel at San Miguel. This may well be the oldest Christian church in the United States. The original building was destroyed in the Pueblo Revolt, but the chapel was rebuilt in 1710.

Old Cienega Village

Tucked into the foothills south of Santa Fe is El Rancho de las Golondrinas (the Ranch of the Swallows). The major attraction is a living history museum called the Old Cienega Village Museum. Walking into the village is like stepping back in time to the 1600s. The village features homes, farm buildings, workshops, a winery, and a water mill. On the first weekends of June, August, and October, artists demonstrate colonial crafts and dances. In June, Civil War buffs gather to reenact a clash between Union and Confederate troops at the Battle of Glorieta.

Coronado State Monument

Just north of Albuquerque, a turn onto Route 44 takes visitors to the Coronado State Monument. The name pays tribute to the explorer Francisco Vásquez de Coronado, who wintered here in 1540. A trail leads through the monument to the Kuaua Pueblo, excavated in the 1930s. Because no one lives here, visitors are allowed to enter the rebuilt kiva to see the colorful frescoes. (Living pueblos such as Zia and Taos bar outsiders from entering their kivas.) As a bonus, the original frescoes can be seen at the visitor center.

Taos Pueblo

After visiting Kit Carson's home in Taos, tourists are encouraged to drive two miles north to Taos Pueblo.

Even though Spanish friars tried to stamp out the making of traditional clay figurines, American Indian potters carried on their work in secret. Each storyteller doll celebrates the custom that calls for tribal elders to pass on their heritage to the children.

Experts say the nine-hundred-year-old pueblo is one of the oldest occupied structures in the United States. In a bow to the modern world, doors have been cut through to most of the rooms. The pueblo's 1,500 Taoseños, however, have drawn the line at wiring the pueblo for electric lights and phones. The quiet settlement springs to joyous life on feast days. Dancers in traditional dress fill the plazas as they celebrate such events as San Juan Day Corn Dance on June 24 and San Geronimo Day trade fair on September 29. Visitors pay a fee to enter, and an additional fee if they want to take photos.

Searching For the Past: California

Most of California's visitors flock to attractions such as Disneyland and Sea World. The Golden State has far more to offer than theme parks, however. The old Royal Highway is gone, but history lives on at the sites it once served. From missions to Gold Rush towns, here are some places that retain the look and feel of the past:

San Diego

A good starting point for a history tour of this seacoast city is the Junípero Serra Museum in Presidio Park. The museum stands on the site of the first mission founded by Father Serra. A collection of artifacts from the city's early history traces its story from 1769 to the present. Walk a few blocks south and you will find Old Town State Historical Park. This collection of restored houses and shops stands on the site of the state's first permanent settlement. To relive the Spanish period, visit Casa de Estudillo. This restored adobe served as a refuge for women and children during the American occupation in 1846. The Wells Fargo History Museum displays an 1865 stagecoach, gold mining gear, and a replica express office. Other attractions include San Diego's first public school and the city's first court-house.

San Juan Capistrano

An easy drive up the Coast Highway takes tourists to the mission town of San Juan Capistrano. The mission, founded by Father Serra in 1776, stands within a walled garden near the center of town. Large crowds gather there on St. Joseph's Day (March 19), hoping to see the first swallows return from their winter homes in Argentina. Towering over the grounds are the ruins of the Great Stone Church, whose dome collapsed in the earthquake of 1812. Visitors can tour the mission buildings and attend services in the restored chapel known as Padre Serra's Church. After leaving the mission, a walk down Los Rios Street takes you past some of the state's oldest homes. If the O'Neill Museum is open you'll see displays of American Indian artifacts and ornate furniture from the 1880s.

A stroll through the gardens of Mission San Juan Capistrano takes visitors back in time. Ever since the Great Stone Church collapsed in the earthquake of 1812, the mission has struggled to regain its former glory.

La Purísima Mission State Historical Park

Farther up the coast a side road leads tourists to the town of Lompoc and Mission La Purísima. Visitors treasure the site for its peaceful country setting and handsome whitewashed buildings. Viewing the scene, it is hard to imagine the ruined, crumbling walls that marked the site when the state bought the land in 1935. Today, La Purísima is said to be the most completely restored of all the missions. Costumed volunteers demonstrate mission crafts in rooms furnished in the style of the 1820s. In the town of Lompoc, California, a small museum displays artifacts left by the Chumash neophytes who helped build the original mission.

Monterey State Historical Park

From Lompoc, a morning's drive up Highway 101 takes you to another page in California's story. Located close to Fisherman's Wharf, Monterey State Historical Park puts the city's rich history on display. Not far from the seven-acre park is the spot where Sebastián Vizcaíno landed in 1602. In 1770, Father Serra stepped ashore on the same spot. From the park, you can take a self-guided "Path of History" tour that leads to a number of historic buildings. Do not miss the Custom House, the oldest government building in California. Back in 1846, Commodore Sloat signaled the end of Mexican rule in California by raising the United States flag over the building.

Wherever traffic is heavy, the old roads have given way to modern multi-lane highways. This same stretch of El Camino Real, now known as Monterey Highway, once carried packtrains north to San Jose.

Columbia State Historical Park

To visit Gold Rush country, leave El Camino Real and drive east and north to Sonora. Another four miles north on Highway 49 takes the visitor to Columbia State Historical Park. For a time, after gold was discovered there in 1850, some twenty thousand miners crowded into the fast-growing town. Then the gold ran out, and Columbia fell into decay until the state restored it in the 1940s. After touring the schoolhouse and the museum, visitors can watch a play at the Fallon House Theater. To end the day, travelers catch up on their sleep at the City Hotel in a room furnished with priceless antiques. In May the old town pulses with life as firemen dragging hand-pumped fire engines gather to compete in the Fireman's Muster.

★ MISSION RECIPES: A GIFT FROM THE PAST ★

No mission tour is complete without a stop to look over the kitchen. Standing in those clean, quiet rooms, it is hard to imagine the tasty dishes that busy cooks once prepared there. For the most part, the food that came to the table was nourishing and plentiful. The recipes came from Spain and Mexico, but over time American Indian cooks added their own touches. The padres must have had a sweet tooth, for many dishes were made with sugar or chocolate. This kitchen-tested dessert recipe will please today's appetites, too.[5]

JIRICALLA (CUSTARD)

The early Californians did not have ice cream, but jiricalla is a close relative.

- 6 eggs
- 1 quart milk

- ¾ cup sugar

- Dash of nutmeg
- ½ cup masa (or 2 table-spoons cornstarch)
- ½ cup water

Separate the eggs and beat the yolks lightly. Scald the milk, add the sugar and nutmeg; then add slowly to the beaten egg yolks. Dilute the masa (the ground corn used to make tortillas) or the cornstarch with the water, blending well. Add the milk-egg mixture and cook over medium heat, stirring all the while, until it thickens. Beat the egg whites until light and fluffy, put on top of the jiricalla; sprinkle sparingly with sugar, place in the oven just long enough to set the meringue. Cool and serve.

THERE ARE NO DANGERS TO TRAVELERS ON THE BEATEN TRACK IN CALIFORNIA; THERE ARE NO INCONVENIENCES WHICH A CHILD OR A TENDERLY REARED WOMAN WOULD NOT LAUGH AT. THEY DINE IN SAN FRANCISCO RATHER BETTER, AND WITH QUITE AS MUCH FORM AND A MORE ELEGANT AND PERFECT SERVICE, THAN IN NEW YORK. THE SAN FRANCISCO HOTELS ARE THE BEST AND CHEAPEST IN THE WORLD. THE NOBLE ART OF COOKING IS BETTER UNDERSTOOD IN CALIFORNIA THAN ANYWHERE ELSE WHERE I HAVE EATEN; THE BREAD IS FAR BETTER, THE VARIETY OF FOOD IS GREATER. THE PERSONS WITH WHOM A TOURIST COMES IN CONTACT, AND UPON WHOM HIS COMFORT AND PLEASURES SO GREATLY DEPEND, ARE MORE UNIFORMLY CIVIL, OBLIGING, HONEST, AND INTELLIGENT THAN THEY ARE ANYWHERE IN THIS COUNTRY. . . . THE COMMON COUNTRY ROADS ARE KEPT IN FAR BETTER ORDER THAN ANYWHERE IN THE EASTERN STATES. AND WHEN YOU HAVE SPENT HALF A DOZEN WEEKS IN THE STATE, YOU WILL PERHAPS RETURN WITH A NOTION THAT NEW YORK IS THE TRUE FRONTIER LAND.

—*CHARLES NORDHOFF, TRAVEL WRITER*[6]

The year was 1873, and Charles Nordhoff worked hard to convince his readers that California was an earthly paradise. Elsewhere in his book, Nordhoff writes that the women of San Francisco pick bouquets from their gardens "the whole year." With their own gardens buried under snow, his eastern readers must have longed to bask in that same western sun.

★ TIMELINE ★

1300 –1325—American Indians launch era of pueblo building along the Rio Grande and its tributaries.

1492—Christopher Columbus opens the Americas to European colonization.

1521—Hernán Cortés conquers Mexico and establishes colony of New Spain.

1540 –1542—Francisco Vásquez de Coronado explores what is now the Southwestern United States.

1540s—El Camino Real de Tierra Adentro is extended north from Mexico City as silver mines open. The route is also known as Camino de la Plata (Silver Road).

1542—Juan Rodríguez Cabrillo explores the California coast as far north as Oregon.

1598—Juan de Oñate opens final leg in El Camino Real de Tierra Adentro, the first road developed by Europeans in what is now the United States.

1602—Sebastián Vizcaíno surveys the California coast, names San Diego and Monterey bays.

1610—El Camino Real de Tierra Adentro reaches newly founded Villa de Santa Fe.

1680—Pueblo Revolt drives Spanish settlers out of New Mexico.

1692—Spanish forces reconquer New Mexico, reopen road to Santa Fe.

1697—Father Salvatierra founds Baja California's first permanent European settlement. His mission at Loreto marks the southern end of California's El Camino Real.

1767—Spain expels Jesuits from New World; Franciscan monks take over missionary role in northern New Spain.

1769—Gaspar de Portolá and Father Serra head north from Loreto to blaze a trail to San Francisco Bay. Serra founds San Diego de Alcalá, Alta California's first mission. The route taken by the party becomes known as El Camino Real.

1770—Father Serra lands at Monterey and chooses the site for his second mission.

1796—The *Otter*, first American ship to visit California, anchors in Monterey Bay.

1810—Mexicans inspired by Father Hidalgo launch a ten-year revolution to free themselves from Spanish rule. Hidalgo later flees north to Chihuahua on El Camino Real de Tierra Adentro.

1821—El Camino Real de Tierra Adentro is given a new lease on life with opening of the Santa Fe Trail between Missouri and New Mexico. Trade surges after Mexico declares its independence.

1823—Father José Altimira founds San Francisco Solano, the twenty-first and last California mission.

1825—California becomes a territory of the new Mexican republic. Traders from the United States bargain with the rancheros for hides, tallow, and sea otter pelts.

1826—Jedediah Smith helps open an overland route to California by forging a key link in what will become the California Trail.

1829—Antonio Armijo and thirty companions travel from Santa Fe to Los Angeles over the Old Spanish Trail in less than ninety days.

1834—Mexico orders the church to turn the missions over to civil authorities.

1846—The Bear Flag Revolt ends Mexican rule in California, but the new flag soon gives way to the Stars and Stripes. As war breaks out between Mexico and the United States, General Kearny takes Santa Fe without firing a shot. United States troops invade Mexico by traveling south on El Camino Real de Tierra Adentro.

1848—James Marshall's discovery of gold in the American River sets off the California Gold Rush. The treaty that ends the Mexican War adds a huge portion of the southwest to the United States.

1850—California joins the Union as the thirty-first state.

1852—Stagecoach service on El Camino Real de Tierra Adentro links Santa Fe, New Mexico, and El Paso, Texas.

1853—Gadsden Purchase adds southern Arizona and New Mexico south of the Gila River to the United States.

1861—Stagecoach service begins between Los Angeles and San Francisco. Another line links El Paso and Los Angeles.

1862—Confederate forces fail in their attempt to drive Union troops out of New Mexico.

1869—The transcontinental railroad carries its first passengers to California.

1881—El Camino Real de Tierra Adentro loses importance as the railroad reaches El Paso.

1906—Mission Bell Association puts up 450 bronze bells to mark El Camino Real. The poorly paved road is better suited to horses than to automobiles.

1909—California Highway Commission uses $18 million bond issue to start construction of a state highway system.

1912—New Mexico admitted to the Union as the forty-seventh state.

1926—California's newly paved coast highway is designated U.S. Highway 101.

1959—California legislature gives Highway 101 official title of El Camino Real.

1995—United States and Mexico lay plans to turn El Camino Real de Tierra Adentro into a national historic trail.

★ CHAPTER NOTES ★

Chapter 1. A Collision of Cultures

1. Douglas Preston and José Antonio Esquibel, *The Royal Road: El Camino Real from Mexico City to Santa Fe* (Albuquerque, N. Mex.: University of New Mexico Press, 1998), p. 3.

2. Ibid., p. 21.

3. Richard B. Morris and the Editors of *Life* magazine, *The New World* (New York: Time, Inc., 1963), p. 42.

4. Douglas Preston, *Cities of Gold: A Journey Across the American Southwest in Pursuit of Coronado* (New York: Simon & Schuster, 1992), p. 301.

5. Olga Hall-Quest, *Conquistadors and Pueblos: The Story of the American Southwest, 1540–1848* (New York: E. P. Dutton, 1969), p. 54.

6. Joshua Paddison, ed., *A World Transformed: Firsthand Accounts of California Before the Gold Rush* (Berkeley, Calif.: Heyday Books, 1999), pp. 12–13.

7. Margot Astrov, ed., *The Winged Serpent: American Indian Prose and Poetry* (Boston: Beacon Press, 1992), p. 271.

8. Hall-Quest, p. 65.

9. Caroline Arnold, *The Ancient Cliff Dwellers of Mesa Verde* (New York: Clarion Books, 1992), p. 61.

10. Zárate Salmerón (trans. by Alicia Ronstadt Milich), *Relaciones* (Albuquerque, N. Mex.: Horn & Wallace Publishers, 1966), pp. 29–30.

11. Ibid., pp. 34–35.

Chapter 2. "Oh God, What a Lonely Land"

1. Olga Hall-Quest, *Conquistadors and Pueblos: The Story of the American Southwest, 1540–1848* (New York: E. P. Dutton, 1969), pp. 70–71.

2. Douglas Preston and José Antonio Esquibel, *The Royal Road: El Camino Real from Mexico City to Santa Fe* (Albuquerque, N. Mex.: University of New Mexico Press, 1998), p. 5.

3. Ibid., p. 6.

4. Max L. Moorhead, *New Mexico's Royal Road: Trade and Travel on the Chihuahua Trail* (Norman, Okla.: University of Oklahoma Press, 1958), pp. 20–21.

5. Ibid., p. 8.

6. Preston and Esquibel, p. 22.

7. Gabrielle G. Palmer, project director, *El Camino Real de Tierra Adentro* (Santa Fe, N. Mex.: Bureau of Land Management, 1993), p. 55.

8. Hall-Quest, p. 107.

9. Preston and Esquibel, p. 172.

10. Palmer, p. 75.

Chapter 3. A New Road in a New Land

1. Edwin Corle, *The Royal Highway (El Camino Real)* (Indianapolis, Ind.: The Bobbs-Merrill Co., 1949), p. 14.

2. Felix Riesenberg, Jr., *The Golden Road: The Story of California's Spanish Mission Trail* (New York: McGraw-Hill Book Co., 1962), p. 15.

3. Ibid., pp. 18–19.

4. Dorothy Krell, *The California Missions: A Pictorial History* (Menlo Park, Calif: Sunset Books, 1979), p. 39.

5. Joshua Paddison, ed., *A World Transformed: Firsthand Accounts of California Before the Gold Rush* (Berkeley, Calif.: Heyday Books, 1999), p. 4.

6. Riesenberg, p. 24.

7. Krell, p. 41.

8. Riesenberg, p. 27.

9. Richard F. Pourade, *The Call to California: The Epic Journey of the Portolá-Serra Expedition in 1769* (San Diego, Calif.: The Union-Tribune Publishing Co., 1968), p. 113.

10. Riesenberg, p. 29.

11. Ibid., p. 32.

12. Carlos Amantea, "Indians in Their Birthday Suits," *The Blob that Ate Oaxaca*, July 1999, <http://www.ralphmag.org/theblob.html> (October 2, 2000).

13. Paddison, pp. 7–8.

Chapter 4. The Mission Trail

1. Ann Roos, *The Royal Road: Father Serra and the California Missions* (Philadelphia: J. B. Lippincott Company, 1951), p. 67.

2. Richard F. Pourade, *Time of the Bells* (San Diego, Calif.: Union-Tribune Publishing Co., 1961), p. 5.

3. Dorothy Krell, *The California Missions: A Pictorial History* (Menlo Park, Calif.: Sunset Books, 1979), p. 46.

4. Felix Riesenberg, Jr., *The Golden Road: The Story of California's Spanish Mission Trail* (New York: McGraw-Hill Book Co., 1962), p. 39.

5. Ibid., p. 40.

6. Krell, p. 316.

7. Spencer Crump, *California's Spanish Missions: Their Yesterdays and Todays* (Corona del Mar, Calif.: Trans-Anglo Books, 1975), p. 34.

8. Riesenberg, p. 34.

Chapter 5. A New Era Dawns

1. Felix Riesenberg, Jr., *The Golden Road: The Story of California's Spanish Mission Trail* (New York: McGraw-Hill Book Co., 1962), p. 63.

2. Richard F. Pourade, *Time of the Bells* (San Diego, Calif.: Union-Tribune Publishing Co., 1961), p. 138.

3. Ibid., p. 140.

4. Max L. Moorhead, *New Mexico's Royal Road: Trade and Travel on the Chihuahua Trail* (Norman, Okla.: University of Oklahoma Press, 1958), pp. 49–51.

5. Riesenberg, p. 65.

6. Ibid., pp. 65–66.

7. Joshua Paddison, ed., *A World Transformed: Firsthand Accounts of California Before the Gold Rush* (Berkeley, Calif.: Heyday Books, 1999), p. 302.

8. Margaret L. Coit and the Editors of *Life* magazine, *The Sweep Westward* (New York: Time Inc., 1963), p. 109.

9. Pourade, pp. 142–143.

10. Ibid.

11. Paddison, pp. 295–297.

12. Francis J. Weber, ed., *The Observations of Benjamin Cummins Truman on El Camino Real* (Los Angeles: Dawson's Book Shop, 1978), p. 25.

Chapter 6. "A Frenzy Seized My Soul"

1. "Santa Fé's Corazón: A Long Marriage, an Enduring Legacy," *Santa Fe*, n.d., <http://www.5520.com/camino-real/santa-fe/index.html> (October 2, 2000).

2. Felix Riesenberg, Jr., *The Golden Road: The Story of California's Spanish Mission Trail* (New York: McGraw-Hill Book Co., 1962), p. 110.

3. Joan M. Jensen and Darlis A. Miller, *New Mexico Women: Intercultural Perspectives* (Albuquerque, N. Mex.: University of New Mexico Press, 1986), p. 72.

4. Richard F. Pourade, *Time of the Bells* (San Diego, Calif.: Union-Tribune Publishing Co., 1961), p. 234–235.

5. Riesenberg, p. 113.

6. Lee Shippey, *It's an Old California Custom* (New York: The Vanguard Press, 1948), pp. 150–151.

7. Dee Brown, *The Gentle Tamers: Women of the Old Wild West* (Lincoln, Nebr.: University of Nebraska Press), p. 204.

8. Edwin Corle, *The Royal Highway [El Camino Real]* (Indianapolis, Ind.: The Bobbs-Merrill Co., 1949), p. 268.

9. Ibid., pp. 270–277.

10. Riesenberg, p. 125–126.

11. Ibid., pp. 126–127.

12. Joshua Paddison, ed., *A World Transformed: Firsthand Accounts of California Before the Gold Rush* (Berkeley, Calif.: Heyday Books, 1999), p. 296.

13. Riesenberg, pp. 147–148.

14. Corle, pp. 289–290.

15. Ibid., pp. 293–294.

16. Shadows of the Past, Inc., "The Story of Charles E. Boles aka Black Bart," *Black Bart the Legend*, 1984–2000, <http://www.sptddog.com/sotp/bbpo8.html> (October 2, 2000).

17. Shippey, p. 146.

18. John Stanchak, "With a Taste for Fine Living and a Weakness for Poetry, 'Black Bart' Confounded Wells Fargo Detectives During an Eight-Year String of Stagecoach Robberies," *Charles 'Black Bart' Boles*, n.d., <http://www.worldwarii.com/AmericanHistory/articles/0682_text.htm> (October 2, 2000).

19. Ibid.

20. Ibid., p. 4.

21. Camino Real Project, "The Expressmen," *El Camino Real: Un Sendero Historico*, n.d., <http://www.millersv.edu/~columbus/data/art/CAMREAL.ART>, p. 24. (October 2, 2000).

Chapter 7. From Gold Rush to Land Boom

1. Lee Shippey, *It's an Old California Custom* (New York: The Vanguard Press, 1948), p. 157.

2. R. R. Olmstead, ed., *Scenes of Wonder & Curiosity from Hutchings' California Magazine, 1856–1861* (Berkeley, Calif.: Howell-North, 1962), pp. 356, 358.

3. Edwin Corle, *The Royal Highway [El Camino Real]* (Indianapolis, Ind.: The Bobbs-Merrill Co., 1949), pp. 306–307.

4. Gabrielle G. Palmer, project director, *El Camino Real de Tierra Adentro* (Santa Fe, N. Mex.: Bureau of Land Management, 1993), p. 209.

5. Corle, p. 310.

6. Ibid., p. 308.

7. Ibid., p. 309.

8. Felix Riesenberg, Jr., *The Golden Road: The Story of California's Spanish Mission Trail* (New York: McGraw-Hill Book Co., 1962), p. 188.

9. Ibid., p. 192.

10. Ibid., p. 204.

11. Francis J. Weber, ed., *The Observations of Benjamin Cummins Truman on El Camino Real* (Los Angeles: Dawson's Book Shop, 1978), p. 38.

12. Pamela Hallan-Gibson, *Ghosts and Legends of San Juan Capistrano* (San Juan Capistrano, Calif.: Pamela Hallan-Gibson, 1983), pp. 20–21.

13. Ibid., p. 13.

14. Riesenberg, p. 204.

Chapter 8. Searching for El Camino Real

1. Douglas Preston and José Antonio Esquibel, *The Royal Road: El Camino Real from Mexico City to Santa Fe* (Albuquerque, N. Mex.: University of New Mexico Press, 1998), p. 34.

2. Ibid.

3. Ghost Team, "Rates of Travel," *Travel in Texas*, n.d., <http://129.115.87.1/projects/tquest/2831/hernando/stravel.htm> (October 2, 2000).

4. Brian Wood and Matt Labovitz, "Mission Report: Santa Barbara; Date: 5/4/95," May 4, 1995, <http://www.tsoft.net/~cmi/Barbara.rpt.html> (October 2, 2000).

5. Recipe borrowed from Dorothy Krell, *The California Missions; a Pictorial History* (Menlo Park, Calif.: Sunset Books, 1979), p. 313.

6. Charles Nordhoff, *California: for Health, Pleasure, and Residence; a Book for Travellers and Settlers* (Berkeley, Calif.: Ten Speed Press, 1973; originally published 1873), p. 18.

★ FURTHER READING ★

Arnold, Carolyn. *The Ancient Cliff Dwellers of Mesa Verde*. New York: Clarion Books, 1992.

Crosby, Harry. *The King's Highway in Baja California: An Adventure Into the History and Lore of a Forgotten Region*. San Diego, Calif.: Copley Press, Inc., 1974.

Krell, Dorothy, ed. *The California Missions: A Pictorial History*. Menlo Park, Calif.: Sunset Books, 1979.

Outland, Charles F. *Stagecoaching on El Camino Real: Los Angeles to San Francisco 1861–1901*. Glendale, Calif.: Arthur H. Clark Co., 1973.

Paddison, Joshua, ed. *A World Transformed: Firsthand Accounts of California Before the Gold Rush*. Berkeley, Calif.: Heyday Books, 1999.

Preston, Douglas and José Antonio Esquibel. *The Royal Road: El Camino Real from Mexico City to Santa Fe*. Albuquerque: University of New Mexico Press, 1998.

Yoder, Walter D. *The Camino Real Activity Book: Spanish Settlers in the Southwest*. Santa Fe: Sunstone Press, 1994.

Internet Addresses

Honig, Sasha, ed. California Mission Studies Association. 1997–2000. <http://www.ca-missions.org> (February 7, 2001).

Mexico Net Guide. El Camino Real de Tierra Adentro. n.d. <http://www.5520.com/camino-real/> (February 7, 2001).

New Mexico Geographic Alliance. Historic Trails and Roads. December 5, 1999. <http://www.nmga.org/nminfo/trails.html> (February 7, 2001).

Wood, Brian. California Missions Interactive. n.d. <http://www.tsoft.net/~cmi/index.html> (February 7, 2001).

★ Index ★